Christmas 1970

© 1961

To Brent:
With all good wishes!
Sincerely,
Rich

The World's Greatest Secret

This figure of a fish was drawn about the
year 150 on the wall of a tomb recently
discovered beneath Saint Peter's Basilica

THE WORLD'S GREATEST SECRET

by

John M. Haffert

Printed in U.S.A.

by

Ave Maria Institute
Washington, New Jersey

FIRST PRINTING - JUNE, 1946 - 4,000 copies (Private Edition distributed for criticism)
SECOND PRINTING - NOVEMBER, 1967 - 20,000 copies (First public distribution)
THIRD PRINTING - SEPTEMBER, 1968 - 10,000 copies (First reprint of corrected edition)

Nihil Obstat
WILLIAM A. MARGERUM, S.T.D.
Censor Librorum

Imprimatur:
✠ GEORGE W. AHR, S.T.D.
Bishop of Trenton

N.B. The Imprimatur implies nothing more than that the material contained herein has been examined by the Diocesan Censor and that nothing contrary to faith or morals has been found therein.

CONTENTS

Chapter

45109

INTRODUCTION

This book is meant for everybody. Maybe that's why some thought it could not be written. we printed four thousand advance copies to survey Protestant, Catholic, and Jewish reaction.

Hundreds helped. Over two hundred sent quotations and ideas; hundreds of others offered daily prayers during the final three years of "production"; and a best-selling author (with a title in the *New York Times'* top ten) spent six months editing the first draft, and another month on the second.

Because it is a book for everybody, it won't satisfy everybody. It will be too cold for the devotional, too skimpy for the professional, too abstruse for the completely uninitiated. For the latter we strongly suggest use of the WORDS, which we have explained at the end in alphabetical order, marked with asterisks throughout the text. For a start, for instance, look up MIRACLE.

Our survey, made to several thousand persons of every shade of knowledge and background, would indicate that the book will be meaningful to most, perhaps even "historic" as many in the survey judged it. If it is, let the glory go to all the unnamed persons who have made it possible. If it is not, may someone more capable have the daring to try again.

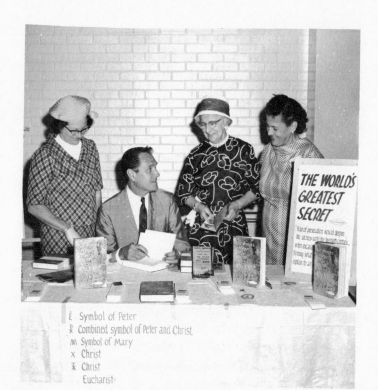

£ · Symbol of Peter
₤ Combined symbol of Peter and Christ
Ɱ Symbol of Mary
x Christ
Ж Christ
Eucharist·

Above the author autographs book at a New Orleans convention while volunteers promoting the book look on. The writer forfeited all royalties so that proceeds from the book are used to distribute it further. Personally convinced by the book, groups of volunteers have organized in most major cities to help make it known. Now in its 30 thousandth copy.

VIII

CHAPTER I

EXCITING DISCOVERY

Near sundown on November 18, 1962, the one-hundred-and-ten ton schooner *Santa Maria* emerged as a speck from the vast sea and splashed her anchor down in twenty feet of water off a tiny Island in the West Indies.

The old ship seemed to sense the thrill of her last great adventure as she rolled in the offshore swell.

We had come to find sunken treasure.

We did. Or at least we found the bones of the Spanish galleon which had broken up on this reef before the United States was born. As in one of those strange stories of pirate maps, we had learned of it somewhat by accident.

But we were not alone.

In the first full daylight we gasped at the sight of the shoreline. Vast craters were scattered over the tiny island. Areas of glaring white coral gaped from the palmetto-covered earth. We were even more amazed to find that one lone man had dug all these craters. He had heard of the galleon apparently many months before we did and had left his family to find it. Now half-mad with treasure lust, long since out of dynamite, he continued to dig frantically with his bare hands. He had become convinced that the survivors of the galleon had removed the bulk of the treasure from the wreck, buried it and died without survivors.

We began to dive on the wreck itself. Down on the ocean floor, breathing through hoses from the surface we found cannon balls and trinkets and coins of centuries ago. We almost forgot our fear of sharks and barracuda under the pressure of tons of water as we became part of America's past.

Just before sundown we used to move the schooner to a cove at the end of the Island. The hours between setting anchor and bedtime were filled with conversations which often had little to do with the treasure. Deeply affected by the sense of solitude, of "other worldliness" experienced together in the silent depths, our thoughts ran to greater things.

The four aboard included a writer who once studied to be a priest; an atheist graduated from Oxford; a professional photographer; and a sailor whose hobbies included weight lifting and skin diving.

The discussions never became angry, but they were often spirited.

"Trouble is," said the Englishman, "you fellows have read too many churchy publications which have prejudiced your judgment. Your church puts the books you ought to read on its index of prohibited books. You probably feel you'd be contaminating

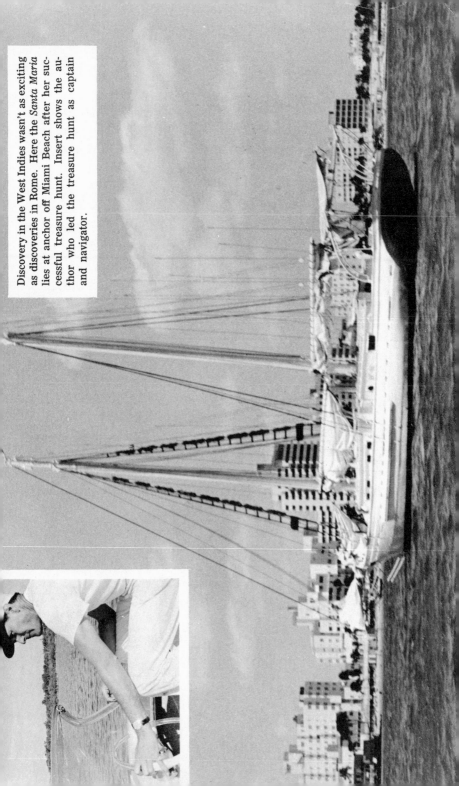

Discovery in the West Indies wasn't as exciting as discoveries in Rome. Here the *Santa Maria* lies at anchor off Miami Beach after her successful treasure hunt. Insert shows the author who led the treasure hunt as captain and navigator.

yourselves if you read Frank Harris* or Henry Miller*. You ride through life in a closed carriage of religious views and never get to know what man really is."

The next day a big barracuda met us over the wreck while we were turning over barnacle-encrusted ballast stones. One of us had felt a "presence" in the water, turned around, and there the great lethal fish hung, staring. We could not know when the lightning speed would be unleashed behind those murderous jaws. One of us signalled that he would watch while the others worked. Our movements became painfully slow. Finally the sailor motioned that he was going to shoot it and the Englishman took up a side position armed only with a short spear.

"That was a brave thing you did," the sailor said to the Englishman as we climbed back on the deck. But the Englishman was always doing brave things. He was one of the finest athletes and most personable companions any of us had ever known. And he did not mean to be rude when he challenged the narrowness of our views, as we also did not mean to be rude when we defended the existence of God. Perhaps without expecting to convince each other, we hoped that some thoughts would sink in like seeds disappearing into swallowing soil, finally conquering it in silence.

*All asterisks refer to WORDS AND REFERENCES in back of book.

"Speaking of Frank Harris," the writer said, "didn't he become an atheist just before he was about to be confirmed in an English boarding school because a Hindu asked him who had made God? And doesn't his autobiography indicate that he rejected God so easily because he didn't like the Commandments?"

Immediately the Englishman defended Harris: "But Frank Harris was a modern Christian. He acknowledged the historic reality of Christ and of the Gospels. Harris was not like the ignoramuses who say Christ never even existed. Himself a great Latin and Greek scholar, he knew of Christ in the writings of Tacitus and of Josephus, contemporary historians. He has a whole chapter in one of his five autobiographical volumes in which he extols Christ, and yet at the same time proves that He was not divine."

Finally we had to leave the wreck for a time because the writer had to return to New York on business for a couple of weeks. He had not known how to answer the challenge that Harris had "proved" Christ was not divine. So he bought a copy of the book, and then was almost as interested in getting back to the schooner to continue those discussions as in continuing the treasure hunt.

Near shipwreck and a host of adventures filled the rest of the voyage, but the discussion at meals and in the few nights of quiet watch still went on. They led to a new and different treasure hunt, and to the writing of this book.

Harris' own words revealed that he first affirmed Christ's reality because of an *archeological** *discovery* which he made in Greece and which, in his own words, "had lent an enormous, *a disproportionate influence on my whole outlook and way of reading the past.*"

He claims that while traveling on foot through Attica he began to wonder about the great ruin of a marble lion which was destroyed by the Turks who thought it contained treasure.

The Turks had found the lion solid. It contained no treasure, and no one had solved the mystery as to why it was standing there.

Harris, who possessed an encyclopedic memory, recalled a great battle which took place on this plain in which three hundred young men of Thebes went out to oppose the invading armies of Philip of Macedon and Alexander. The three hundred young men had taken a solemn oath to stop the invaders or die in the attempt. They were all killed. Plutarch, who described the event, mentioned a river on the plain. Harris says that he studied the area and while there was now no river, a shallow brook flowed not far from the fragments of the lion and a long, grass-grown depression. He reasoned that the lion had been a memorial over the tomb.

He persuaded archeologists* to excavate in that particular spot. They found four stone walls a foot or so broad and six feet or so in height, built in the form of an elongated square, resting on the shingle of an old river bed. Inside there were 297 skeletons. In a corner was a little pile of ashes which they took to be the remains of the other three who had survived longest and were finally cremated. Evidence of the terrible conflict was still discernible in the condition of the skeletons, one of which had three ribs smashed on one side, while the head of a spear was found jammed between another rib and a backbone; another backbone had been broken by a vigorous spear thrust and one side of the head beaten in as well.

Had it not been for the account in Plutarch, which Harris remembered, the ruin of a lion might still be a mystery.

Previously this description of the battle by Plutarch had been taken by many to be poetic legend.

"I began to read other books," Harris writes, "and notably the New Testament, in a different spirit. German scholars had taught me that Jesus was a mythical figure: His teachings a mishmash of various traditions and religions and myths. He was not an historical personage in any way, they declared; the three synoptic Gospels were all compiled from fifty to eighty years after the events, and John was certainly later still."

Harris, although an atheist, now became convinced of the historical reality of Christ because he now knew from personal experience that records of history do not diminish in accuracy because of age. A record of 2000 years ago could be just as accurate as a description written yesterday. Not only have the facts of Christ's life been told by four different companions (Matthew, Mark, Luke and John), who even offered their lives in testimony of what they recorded, but the same reality of Christ was confirmed by other contemporary historians such as Josephus and Tacitus.

Now convinced of the fact of Christ, how did Harris, the atheist, react? How did he "prove" Christ was not divine?

Admitting that Christ appeared to hundreds of persons after allegedly dying on the cross, Harris says that Christ had merely fainted, and that afterward because of the care of those who were waiting He was able to be brought back to health and to show Himself to His disciples. Harris says: "If He were dead, He must have been dead for some time, the time at least necessary for someone to go to Jerusalem and see Pilate and return again to Calvary with the order to test the apparent death."

It is remarkable that Harris felt himself to be one of the world's greatest scholars, perhaps because he could memorize whole passages so easily and could speak six languages. *Yet he did not know how far*

Calvary was from the Fortress Antonia where Pilate presided that day!

The distance from Calvary to Fortress Antonia is only a ten-minute walk. On horseback around the wall, as it was then, it could have been no more than a few minutes!

Anchored off the Island of San Salvador, where Columbus' extraordinary landfall exploded the world into a new age, the writer quietly summed up to the atheist: "You accuse believers of prejudice and ignorance, but it is usually the other way about."

The writer had traveled around the Mediterranean just before the treasure hunt and he knew of some exciting discoveries, especially in Rome.

"If Harris could be convinced about the facts of Christ because he found a grave in a field in Greece, even as we came alive to early American history when we found pieces-of-eight among the bones of a Spanish galleon, I think we should be able to find something better than a Grecian grave to help good men realize that there is something more glorious than Henry Miller's "pus and open sewers", something better to which to look forward than your new prophets like Maupassant slitting his own throat in his early forties.

So we began to wonder: what is the buried secret of a Spanish galleon when compared to the secrets now being uncovered by scientific, well-equipped treasure hunters of history: the modern archeologists?* When we see the vastness of their

excavations spreading around the entire Mediterranean and get some inkling of the scientific precision with which they work to uncover the secrets
of the past, does not the common sea-going treasure
hunter seem like a haphazard amateur looking for
baubles?

For five years prior to finding the wrecked galleon, our imagination had been captivated by the
reported archeological findings around the Mediterranean area, particularly in Rome. Now, with the
success of discovering the bones of a Spanish ship we
began to wonder: Why not go to Italy to verify those
archeological finds? The Spanish galleon had seemed
like a myth until we felt those pieces of eight in our
hands. And if we could verify a rumor by merely
lifting real coin from the bottom of the sea, where
we had only half expected to find it, then why
shouldn't we hope to verify that far more precious
coin of the world's greatest secret which modern
archeologists claimed to have discovered?

So the Santa Maria was returned to Miami and
her skipper boarded an ocean liner to spend most of
the next two years in Europe writing this book.

Those Mediterranean treasure hunters with pick
and shovel knew where to look. Their knowledge of
history has leaped ahead during recent years. Documents have been found, catalogued, duplicated on
microfilm and made available to them at stations
around the world. They found Pompeii. They found

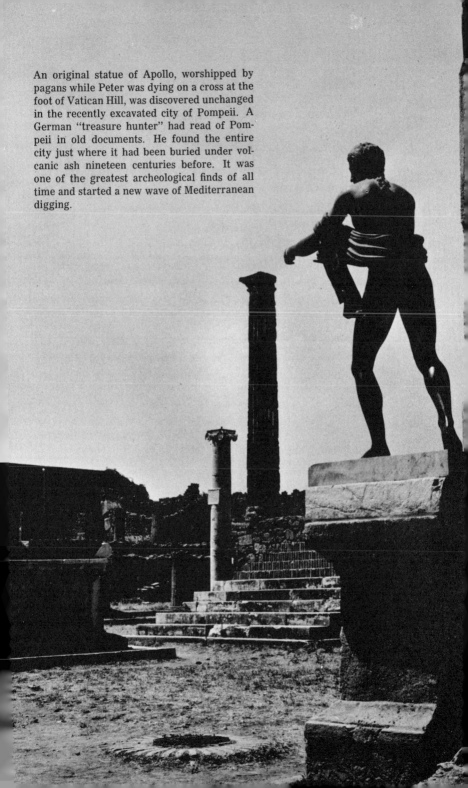

An original statue of Apollo, worshipped by pagans while Peter was dying on a cross at the foot of Vatican Hill, was discovered unchanged in the recently excavated city of Pompeii. A German "treasure hunter" had read of Pompeii in old documents. He found the entire city just where it had been buried under volcanic ash nineteen centuries before. It was one of the greatest archeological finds of all time and started a new wave of Mediterranean digging.

Herculaneum and Capharnaum and dozens of other ancient cities long since drowned beneath the waves of the changing earth.

Back in that schooner in the West Indies we began to understand the modern archeologists because we knew with advance precision about the galleon whose bones we picked.

Most of the greatest archeological finds of our time have been similarly made because of old documents. It was long known, for example, that probably an important cemetery of the First Century was still uncovered in Rome. And cemeteries, to treasure hunters of civilization, are more exciting than the smell of gold to treasure hunters of the sea. Cemeteries contain tombs, and ancient tombs with their pottery, coins, and inscriptions are time-capsules of the past.

Unfortunately, most of the cemeteries of Rome had been emptied before the archeologists reached them. After the Roman Empire crumbled, wave upon wave of invaders pillaged mausoleums and catacombs.

But ancient documents spoke of an important cemetery on Vatican Hill.

There was every reason to believe that while the original church over the cemetery had been destroyed, the cemetery itself never had been found, never had been pillaged. It might indeed be intact!

In 1900, by unanimous vote, the International

This vast structure presented no small problem to the scientists who wanted to excavate under it. From the back, (behind us, out of the picture) St. Patrick's Cathedral in New York would fill the space only as far as the top of the curve in the crowd where the Swiss guards block the aisle. The church will hold the entire population of a small city (25,000).

Archeologists' Congress petitioned Pope Leo XIII
to excavate beneath the church.

But the Pope refused. The church in question
was Saint Peter's Basilica, the largest church in the
world!

In 1939, an accident led to discovery.

Pope Pius XII, the reigning pontiff at that time,
had ordered a portion of the floor of Saint Peter's
crypt lowered to receive the tomb of Pius XI, and a
workman fell through. It must have been a little like
Alice's falling through the rabbit hole. He landed in
a different world: in a first century cemetery.

With that, the excavation was on.

The expense resembled a U.S. government ap-
propriation. Several superstructures, though "modern" in comparison to the substructures, had been
built long before Columbus discovered America.
They had to be shored up. The dome rose above
that very spot almost as high as a forty story sky-
scraper!

This vast structure almost as tall as the Time
and Life Building in New York, with a "wing" so
big it could be used for a football stadium, presented
problems to the scientists who wanted to dig beneath it. It had taken one hundred and twenty years
to build. Nobody wanted it to come crashing down
in as many seconds, even to probe the secrets of the
past!

Painstakingly, slowly, the work proceeded. Excitement and suspense mounted. Excavators hit a rich religious lode and began to discover things hidden since Constantine built the first basilica on the same spot back in the year 315.

They were still tallying the finds when Pius XII died in 1958, twenty years after the first archeological spade sank questingly between the great foundations.

The cemetery they found dated from the time of Christ. Some tombs were found so perfectly preserved that the mosaic and fresco decorations seemed brand new. Excavations from the central floor of the basilica slowly worked toward the spot where tradition said that Peter had been buried.

Almost at once two surprising facts came to light:

First, some of the pagan tombs of the first century had been filled in during the 4th century by the then-pagan Emperor, Constantine[1], to serve as foundations of a Christian church. This was particularly amazing because the pagan Romans had an almost superstitious respect for tombs. In all history only twice did Roman emperors violate the catacombs, even during ruthlessly thorough persecutions. Obviously the pagan Emperor must have had a very pressing reason for allowing some tombs to be filled for building foundations.

[1] Constantine, though he declared himself in favor of Christianity earlier, was not himself baptized until shortly before his death, and was therefore a pagan when he built the first "St. Peter's Basilica" on Rome's Vatican Hill.

Second, as the excavators approached that area where Peter was said to be interred, they found Christian tombs squeezed among the pagan tombs in increasing numbers. They even found some Christians buried in the older pagan mausoleums which were there before Peter's death.

Most amazing was the discovery of Peter's grave.

It was a very poor tomb, lowered in the ground, sealed with a slab of stone. Ordinarily it would never have attracted any attention . . . squeezed as it was between magnificent pagan mausoleums.

Because of their immense respect for the dead, the Romans had never desecrated Peter's tomb, despite the increasingly bitter persecutions of Christians. They had done the next thing: They had tried to camouflage or hide it. They had built a staircase from one level of the cemetery to an upper level right over this tomb. The date of this staircase was ascertained from a marked tile in its foundation. The staircase was built less than a century after Peter's death, when Christianity was beginning to spread like a consuming fire through the pagan world. The red staircase wall, which had been built within the life span of a single man after Peter's crucifixion, was covered with a maze of inscriptions.

The first archeologists to see this wall found most of the markings as undecipherable as hieroglyphics had been before the discovery of the Rosetta Stone.* Pius XII, who had undertaken the task of

It must have been a little like Alice's falling through the rabbit hole. He landed in a different world: in a first century cemetery.

the excavations, did not live to see their major translations. Experts began to identify these inscriptions
with similar ones which had begun to turn up in
excavations all over the Mediterranean area in Christian tombs of the first and second centuries. These
markings partially lifted the curtain on early Christian beliefs.

Before the meaning of the red wall markings
was deciphered, workmen made other finds. They
found three altars directly below the 16th century
altar which visitors see today beneath the dome of
St. Peter's. Each altar is on a different level, one
above the other, having been built at about 500-year
intervals. The most recent had been built by Callixtus, the next by Gregory the Great, and the last and
earliest by Constantine who was the first of the Roman emperors to recognize Christianity.

The altar of Constantine crowded out still a
fourth altar, a 'trophy' with two columns and a sort
of trapdoor underneath it. The 'trophy' was built
into the staircase wall which bore the many inscriptions.

One of the inscriptions, older than the enclosure
of Constantine, reads: "PETER LIES WITHIN".
The name and symbol of Peter were found everywhere about. One line scribbled about 150 A.D.
reads: "Paccius Eutychus remembered Glycon here."
In the eighteen centuries since then how many pilgrims to Peter's tomb have written home:

Painstakingly, slowly, the work progressed.

"I remembered you here."

Why had Pius XII reversed the decision of his predecessors and agreed, at such tremendous risk and expense, to unearth Peter's tomb? Was he trying to produce a creditable witness for Christ? Or did he guess we might find some evidence of Christ's doctrinal legacy for which Peter had been willing to die? It might help us to understand if we translate what happened to Peter into modern context.

Rome in its prime, was like Washington or Moscow today. If our world were pagan and Christ came now, what would happen if a creditable, intelligent witness traveled to Washington to testify about Him before a joint session of Congress?

Since Christ performed great miracles, converting thousands and thereby upsetting the traditions underlying all contemporary life, Congress might listen, and might even be more tolerant than were Caligula, Claudius or Nero.

But suppose the witness had been forced to go to Moscow or Peking? Could he have expected any better treatment than Peter and Paul expected in Rome?

So this digging under the great Roman basilica to the tomb of Christ's "witness"*was a dramatic, scientific step into Christianity's infancy. It was a direct contact with an important witness of Christian faith.

Some of the pagan tombs of the first four centuries had been filled in . . . an amazing fact because it was a pagan emperor who ordered it done.

After all, the writings and the spoken words of Christ's later followers have often been confusing. Over two hundred Christian sects have grown out of different interpretations of the Gospels.

So which teachings of Christ most impressed Peter, a man who walked with Christ, learned directly from His lips, and died at last for his belief in what he had heard Christ teaching?

Because they partially answer this question, the inscriptions on the wall over Peter's tomb were truly the *great* discovery made in our own time . . . a discovery vastly more exciting than a pile of cannon balls and some pieces of eight or the remains of three hundred Thebans in an Attica grave.

Mausoleums, or tombs, were found in almost perfect state. The second amazing fact was that clustered around the tomb of Peter were squeezed tombs of Christians, some even inside the pagan mausoleums.

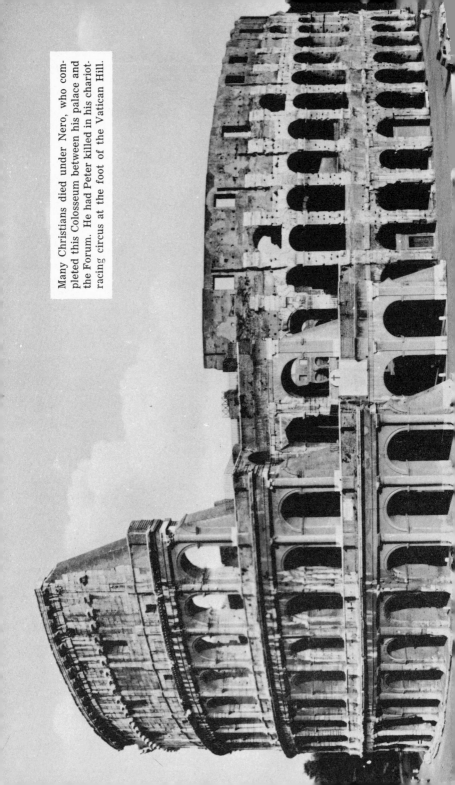

Many Christians died under Nero, who completed this Colosseum between his palace and the Forum. He had Peter killed in his chariot-racing circus at the foot of the Vatican Hill.

CHAPTER II

WHY THE SECRECY?

THE EARLY CHRISTIANS lived in a clandestine church set against a backdrop of fear. They would slink through underground passages, performing religious rites deep in the bowels of the earth where pagan eyes could not penetrate.

The reason lies in one terrible word: persecution. Only understanding of that word can enable us to grasp why the subject of this book first became the world's greatest secret.

The horrors of early century persecutions have been recorded in various documents beginning with the Bible itself: In the Acts there is a description of the stoning of Stephen, and later St. Paul in his epistles refers to the persecutions in Rome. At the time that Paul wrote, persecutions were still a comparatively new phenomenon, and they were not quite so thorough as they subsequently became. Paul himself was able to preach openly in the Imperial City (though under custody) for two years before he was beheaded.

Tertullian, writing in the second century, gives

us an inkling of the persecutions which Nero inaugurated.

Then the writer Pliny paints a wider picture. It was he whom Emperor Trajan sent to the Province of Bithynia-Pontus to quell "disorder" reported there. He writes that he was amazed to find that a large percentage of the Province had become Christian. This caused "disorder" because the members of the new religion no longer brought animal victims for sacrifice to the gods, and dealers in animals felt the economic pinch, as did the pagan priests.

Pliny asked the Emperor how he should handle the matter and Trajan's reply, recorded by Pliny, became the basis for persecution of Christians until Constantine became emperor in 313, and briefly afterward in the reign of Julian the Apostate. The decree of Trajan demanded that Christians recant and offer sacrifice to the gods or die. Shortly after this the staircase and wall were built over Peter's tomb in the cemetery on Vatican Hill.

Does all this seem like a fantastic tale from some Never-Never Land only dimly discernible beyond the mists and shadows of time?

To us of the twentieth century, it should seem more real than that. We are no strangers to persecution. It rages virulent and violent and vicious all about us.

Father Leopold Braun, A.A., for many years pastor of the one Roman Catholic church within the borders of the USSR[1] said that he did not keep baptismal or marriage records. The Cheka, or secret police, who appeared unexpectedly from time to time to inspect his files, would have visited reprisals on his parishioners had he kept such records.

Then Father Robert Greene, M.M., who was a missionary in the little village of Tung-an in south China tells his experiences in his book CALVARY IN CHINA. When the Reds took over in 1950, one of their first acts was to paint on the side of the church in huge characters, words reading "Freedom of Religion."

Seeing this, the happy parishioners thronged to the church as usual for Sunday Mass. As they entered the door Communist soldiers stood aside and watched.

A few nights later, the priest lying awake in his bed heard sounds beneath his window. He looked out. Red soldiers were marching by, leading a civilian prisoner.

In the morning he was told: " 'Old Lee Tu-pao was taken from his home last night and no one knows what has happened to him.' "

Eventually the church building was used as a prison where Red soldiers questioned the unfortunates and "encouraged" them to "confess." Father

---

[1] Father Braun was allowed in the Soviet Union when the United States granted the country diplomatic recognition.

Green describes the glimpse he had of it one day.[1]
"Two men strung up by their thumbs to a hook on
the wall, their toes barely touching the floor . . .
I know of one Christian who went eight days thus
strung up before he eventually died."

Naturally, the Christians lived in a nightmare
of suspense and dread. Father Greene hid the Blessed
Sacrament in his bookcase. To make matters worse,
he distrusted his own former parishioners, and parents distrusted their own children.

A similar fear and distrust exists in East Germany. The February 1966 Bulletin of St. Ignatius
church, San Francisco, published an excerpt from
a letter written by a priest in East Berlin. A woman
came to him and asked: "My son wants to flee to
West Germany to study engineering. Should I let
him go?"

The priest ponders in his letter: "Is the woman's
problem genuine, or does she have 'the task' of exposing me as 'an instigator of defection'?"

Dr. Thomas Dooley tells of the terrible persecution of Christians in Vietnam in his immortal book
Deliver Us from Evil. And in his book, *The Night
They Burned the Mountain,* Dr. Dooley tells of his
fears when confronted with the thought that he
might have to abandon his crew of Asian workers

[1] —Page 88 of CALVARY IN CHINA, published by G. P. Put-
man's Sons, N. Y 1953

and leave Laos before the Communist invasion:

"I knew that the six or eight of my star pupils would be taken out and beheaded in front of the whole village and their heads, with the organs of the neck hanging down, would be impaled upon stakes. I knew that the Communists would take members of my Lao crew, stand them in a circle facing inward, and with machetes would deftly cut the tendons in the back of their knees. When the crew would fall to the ground the Communists would walk around and hack them to pieces. I have seen the Communists do this and just leave the men in the middle of a room or in a field. When the tendons were cut, the Lao would not bleed to death. They would crawl like animals until they were caught and hacked to death. This is what they would do to Chai, to Si, to Ngoan, and to Deng. To the girls on my staff they would do even more dreadful things."

But the mind boggles at the hideous facts. We find that we are thinking of them as if they were the stuff of an Alfred Hitchcock TV skit which had somehow gone awry; we can scarcely realize that they are actual occurrences on this familiar planet, Earth.

Horror is always difficult to grasp whether it is of ancient Rome, of present-day Communist regimes, or for that matter of yesterday's Nazism which took the lives of thousands. Who will forget the awful drama of day to day secrecy which fills the diary of Anne Frank, a secrecy which only postponed the agony of the gas chamber?

Only twenty-four hours after the arch-Nazi, Adolph Eichmann, had been hanged the present writer drove past the chalk walls of the prison in Israel where the hanging occurred. All was quiet. If the wretch had cried out as he fell through the trap, no echo resounded from the quiet hills. It was as though the grisly deed of his hanging and all his own grisly deeds had never taken place. Peaceful green fields lay beneath the shadow of the timeless Palestinian hills. Christ saw those same fields—so the mind darts off on a tangent, seeking a pleasant, romantic thought. We wondered then: if we find it difficult to realize the monstrosity of an Eichmann who died here *yesterday,* can we ever realize the grim persecutions of *two thousand years ago?*

However, it helps a little to have the cryptographic writings. They are tangible evidence. And we find cryptography* in abundance not only on Peter's tomb, and under the basilica of St. Peter's church, but also in a first century room discovered in 1915 under St. Sebastian's church beyond the walls of Rome.[1]

---

[1] Although excavations were not completed until 1956, and are still the subject of study, the original discovery was made by Dr. P. Styger in 1915. See also A TRAVELER IN ROME, by H. V. Morton, pg. 144; THE TOMBS OF SS PETER AND PAUL, by E. Kirschbaum, pg. 196.

FREQUENTLY RECURRING SYMBOLS AROUND PETER'S TOMB:

Symbol of Peter combines P and E and also forms image of a key, recalling Christ's words to Peter: "I will give to thee the keys to the kingdom of Heaven." (Matt. XVI, 19)

Combined symbol of Peter and Christ.

Symbol of the name of Mary.

It took experts several years to "pick apart" the heavy inscriptions, one on top of the other, which covered the red wall over Peter's tomb.

The symbols and the writings, meaningless to an outsider, like a lightning flash back over the centuries reveal how the early Christians lived.

Looking at the modern-day Christians in China we know what that meant. The Christians of the little town of Tung-an knew that discovery would lead to the firing-squad—or much worse. In some cases, they were in fear not only for themselves but also for the people who sheltered them, so they exercised the caution of hunted animals. They used every form of concealment, reticence, and seclusion; they created every barrier, curtain, purdah, shade, mask or disguise that ingenuity could devise.

Obviously, it was the same for the early Christians. To become a Christian in the first centuries meant to choose concealment as a way of life. Fear was a cloak that one donned along with the symbolic white robe of Baptism. The poor creature was henceforth hedged about with countless inhibitions, lest a word, a gesture, or some tiny act of his give him or his friends away.

The catacombs, fetid, cold and damp were the meeting-places of the brethren. There they could perform their religious rites hidden from hostile gaze, and protected by the Romans' superstitious respect for cemeteries.

In this atmosphere of secrecy the Christians hid their beliefs in symbols, and archeologists today study those symbols for answers. As far back as the fourth century, historians called Christian life "the discipline of the secret." However, much earlier, before it was called anything at all, it was a deeply ingrained discipline. It was so much a part of Christianity that it could not be shuffled off even after the need for it no longer existed. Secrecy survived in the East until the fifth century, in the West until the sixth. It took time for people to believe that the persecutions were really over and done with. For a long time there was a latent fear of renewal.

When partially trusted strangers or new converts from paganism attended Christian rites, they were allowed to stay only for the first part of the prayers and ceremonies. They were required to leave when the second, more private part was about to begin. The first part of the liturgical* service was designated for "the catechumens" (that is for those still learning the catechism of the Faith) and the rest designated for "the faithful" (that is for those who had proved their steadfastness in the Faith and had been baptized). The great ACT of the liturgy of "the faithful" was perhaps the most carefully guarded secret of all history. To this day in the liturgy it was referred to as "the secret" until 1964!

This secret so filled the hearts and minds of the first Christians that archeologists and historians working all around the Mediterranean keep uncovering the secret symbols day after day. Early Christians had not been afraid to express the secret in symbols and pictures because unless a man knew the secret, the symbols would be meaningless. The secret was *too mystic for mere humans to guess*. Indeed, it was almost too mystic for humans to believe. After Vatican Council II removed the label of secrecy and openly substituted "Liturgy of the Eucharist" for "Secret," the mystery began to creep into interfaith dialogue. The current sound and excitement seems to echo what was heard when Christ first announced it.

CHAPTER III

BEGAN AS A SECRET

IT MAY HAVE BEEN the most terrible moment that the apostles ever experienced; more terrible than Gethsemane or Calvary; even more terrible than the moments of their own deaths.

They had left all to follow Christ. They had turned their backs upon their wives, children, their homes, businesses—everything. They had thought that nothing mattered except what He did, what He said. They were convinced that He would lead them to reward, to great triumph. They expected Him to establish His kingdom soon, and they, His chosen companions and intimates, wearing purple and scarlet, would be His administrators. Indeed, judging from the crowds, the time was ripe now, today.

They were near the bustling town of Capharnaum. Just about every inhabitant of the place had turned out to hear Him speak. The people followed Him with a breathless eagerness all the way up the hill overlooking the lake.

Moreover, since the Pasch was at hand, people on holiday from neighboring hamlets were gathered here for the approaching feast, or they were on their way to the great temple in Jerusalem. The apostle Matthew who had been an accountant, estimated that there were five thousand men alone, excluding women and children. The grassy hillside was black with humanity.

Christ did not disappoint them. He spoke to them with greater eloquence than ever; quietly, forcefully, and every man, bright-eyed and intent, leaned forward listening as though his life depended upon the next word.

The meal hour came and went and scarcely a person in that vast throng gave it a thought. Only as He finished His discourse did the people become aware of a gnawing in the pit of their stomachs, and it was then they noticed for the first time that many of the children were crying fretfully and asking for bread.

It had not occurred to the townsfolk to bring food with them when they had followed Him up the hill. Perhaps subconsciously they had considered that precaution unnecessary. As long as He was with them hunger, accident, illness, nothing would bother them.

The apostles were concerned. Though they felt a bit presumptuous to tell Him a fact that He must know, they reminded Him: "This is a desert place. Send the people away so that they can buy their dinner."

Christ's answer was strange:

Ruins of the Synagogue in Capharnaum where Christ stunned the crowd with His "incredible" statement.

"Give them something to eat."

Did He mean that they should empty their little treasury and make the round trip to town to buy the scant rations their funds would provide? He asked the apostle Philip: "Where can we buy bread that these people may have something to eat?"

Philip's answer seems almost impatient: "Two hundred pennyworth, which is the most we could muster, wouldn't buy a crumb for everybody here."

"How many loaves have you?" Christ asked.

Of course they had no loaves at all. Nobody in that huge crowd had anything edible but one young lad. Andrew, another apostle, pointed out the boy: "That lad over there has five barley loaves and two fishes. But," the man added with a shrug, "what is that among so many?"

"Bring them to me," Christ said simply.

When Christ had the bread and fish before Him, he bade the people sit down. Then He looked up to heaven, blessed the food, and handed it to the apostles, instructing: "Give it to the people."

As the twelve men passed among the huge crowd, serving one hungry person after another, they soon noticed a strange phenomenon: the food they carried never diminished.

There was always plenty for the next person, and the next, and the next. In the end there was more than enough for each one of those many thousands to eat heartily, and when the meal was over the apostles gathered up *twelve baskets of left-overs.*

Slowly the people began to grasp the marvel. They understood that this man, this carpenter's son, this Jesus Christ, had miraculously by an act of His will or a wave of His hand or a mumbled prayer or whatever, miraculously multiplied a few scraps of food, making them enough to satisfy the appetites of somewhere between five and fifteen thousand hungry people.

He was a prophet all right, and more than a prophet. He was a Wonderworker beyond their wildest dreams. With Him as their leader there need be no more hunger in Israel. The Romans themselves with all their proud legions would cringe before such power.

As they commented to one another excitement mounted. Somebody had scarcely voiced the suggestion of making Him king when a lusty cheer went up on all sides. The crowd was of one mind: they would seize Him where He stood and forthwith proclaim His sovereignty.

But where was He?

He Who wished to be king only of the hearts of men had slipped away.

It was the next day when they came upon Him again. They jostled one another in their eagerness to get close to Him. Expectation was alight on every face, but it was quickly dimmed by His first words.

They seemed almost a rebuke: "You looked for me not because you have seen my other miracles or because you seek the things of the spirit, but only because I fed you."

The apostles, too, were chagrined and nonplussed by these words, and did not quite know how to answer. He went on: "You should strive not for the meat which spoils quickly, but for the meat which lasts into eternity. I, the Son of Man, will give you that meat."

That sounded better. But it was still puzzling. Some people in the crowd a little bolder than the rest, asked: "How do we get this food?"

"I will tell you," Christ replied. "Believe in Me. I have been sent by your Father in heaven."

"All right, we'll believe," a number of people shouted. "But," added a few of them "show us a sign."

Apparently they wanted another miracle like yesterday's or one even more spectacular. After all, as one man pointed out to his neighbors, now that he had slept on the matter, the feat of this Wonderworker with the bread and fish did not seem so great to him as it had at first. Some prophets of the past had wrought similar marvels. In fact, the man challenged Christ outright: "Our fathers ate manna in the desert. That was miraculous food, too."

Yes, Moses had fed the people for forty years on manna in the Sinai desert, and this Christ had fed them only once. Even the apostles remembered about that, and they nodded their heads when somebody quoted the scriptural text referring to the patriarch: "He gave them bread from heaven."

Christ's response was: "Moses gave you not the true bread from heaven, not the bread from heaven like the kind that my Father will give you. *This new bread which comes from heaven will give life to the world.*"

With these promising words a clamor arose: "We want this bread! We want this bread!"

"I myself am the bread of life," Christ answered. "Whoever comes to Me will never again be hungry, and whoever believes in me will never again be thirsty."

A clearly audible murmur ran through the crowd. What was He talking about? He Himself the bread of life! He, the son of Joseph the carpenter, come down from heaven! Didn't everybody for miles around know His father and mother?

"Don't murmur among yourselves. Rather believe my words," Christ pleaded. "The man who has faith in Me shall receive eternal life. It is I Who am the Bread of Life. Though your fathers ate manna, they nevertheless died. But," he went on, repeating Himself now as though He were telling them the one thing above all others that He really wanted them to heed and remember, "whoever eats

the true bread from heaven shall never die. If anybody eats this bread he will live forever."

He paused as though for dramatic effect, and
then said slowly: *"This bread which I am going to
give you is my flesh."*

A gasp went up from the crowd. What a hard
saying! It was repellent . . . disgusting. The apostles
who loved and trusted Him were visibly shaken. They
looked at one another as though to ask if they had
heard correctly.

But the crowd was in an uproar. The people
were arguing noisily, returning time and again to the
same refrain: "How can this man give us His flesh
to eat?" But they took care lest Jesus should hear
their doubts.

In the past He had often restated a point that
had been misinterpreted. Now He remained silent.
So were they to take him literally? They could hardly think otherwise, for when He did speak again it
was only to insist solemnly on what He had said before, and indeed to say it more emphatically. "Believe Me when I say that you cannot have life, you
cannot be alive, unless you eat the flesh of the Son
of Man and drink His blood. The person who eats
my flesh and drinks my blood will have eternal life
and I will raise him up on the last day. My flesh is
real food, and my blood is real drink. Whoever eats
my flesh and drinks my blood lives always in and
with Me and I in and with him."

This was just too much! The people shook

their heads, and then one by one turned away. Though a few hours earlier they had been willing to revolt against the established government for His sake, and as revolutionaries had been willing to risk the danger of Herod's armies—not to speak of the Roman legions—now they would not listen to Him another moment. Their great bravery in being willing to hail a king other than Caesar had come to naught. It had been demolished by the mouthings of a mad man.

The apostles saw the people drift off. It was their kingdom, too, which was disappearing before it was established—more their kingdom than it was this crowd's. Again they could not help reminding themselves that they would have been its administrators under Christ. The glorious prize had been within their grasp. And now? With each departing figure their hopes sank lower. Finally they were left alone with Him. Even one of them should have left also, because he, like the crowd, had repudiated the Master in his heart. St. John points out (6:65) "Jesus knew which were those who did not believe and which of them would betray Him."

This sensitive person, Jesus Christ, Who was later so touched with compassion at the sorrow of Martha and Mary that He wept with them, must have been touched by the sadness and disappointment that He saw in the faces of His disillusioned followers. He must have longed at that moment to explain away this apparently cannibalistic thing He had said.

But He did not explain it away; He didn't even explain it. He simply said:

"The words I have just spoken here today are spirit and life. Do they try your faith?"

Of course they would try anybody's faith! But like abashed school boys without the proper answer, the apostles stood there nervously shuffling their sandaled feet on the ground, and not one of them spoke up. Christ had to put them to the test with another question:

"Will you, too, go away?"

Still they hesitated to speak. But before the silence lengthened too agonizingly Peter stepped forward. He had not understood any better than anybody else, but he believed in the Master and that was enough. "To whom could we go?" he asked. Then with a stronger voice to sweep away any lingering doubt he added in a spontaneous burst: "You Lord, have the words of eternal life. We believe, we know that You are the Christ, Son of God."

Whatever the awesome secret Christ implied in His daring statement, apparently no one was ready to grasp it. He let an earthly kingdom slip away rather than yet reveal it.

But the Israelites had many clues. Their Scriptures spoke of a Saviour who would come, Who would be linked with the mystery of the Passover, and Who would reveal all.

CHAPTER IV

THE CURTAIN WOULD FALL

WHEN HARRIS PROBED a grave in an empty field in Greece to verify that three hundred Thebans had died there, it was difficult to realize that two thousand years ago this was an important part of the world.

Today man is spread around the globe. But, then, with the exception of scattered barbarian tribes and a pocket of culture in the Orient, those few countries around the Mediterranean Sea were *the world*.

And the heart of that world was not so much Rome and Athens, which were cities busy with politics and northern barbarism. Even more, it would now appear, the heart of the world was where civilization seems to have begun: About in the area where Christ made His incredible announcement.

Over three million persons lived around that small Lake of Galilee. It was a major center of population. Famous Greek cities known as the decapolis extended the Greek civilization down from Athens on one side of the Lake, and on the other the richest cultural and social heritage of Ancient Egypt was found wedded in the enlightened Hebrews to whom Christ spoke.

45

What impelled them, even after an entire night during which to ponder the drastic consequences, to proclaim Him their king? Was it only because he had fed them?

He had no army! Could he defend them in their opposition to the might of Rome? Were not his mere twelve men as poor and inconsequential as the twelve baskets of remains from the bread and fish? Yet they had made up their minds. They wanted Him to be their King.

We know there was an air of royalty about Him, and power. Later a Roman governor was impulsively to ask, and without humor: "Are you a king?" And the soldiers were not joking later when they felt an impulse to mock him as a king, then blindfolded those eyes that flashed regality and power. He was a man who seemed to fit a description given by one of their own most venerable prophets, Jeremias: *A man of contradiction.*

That same prophet had foretold the captivity of the Jews, their deliverance, and finally the coming of a saviour who would make their glorious delivery from Egypt a mere shadow of the deliverance and security He would bring: "In those days shall Juda be saved, and Jerusalem shall dwell securely; and this is the name they shall call Him: The Lord, or just one." (Jer. 33,v7-16)

That day by the Sea of Galilee they suspected

that He was the Saviour of whom Jeremias and their other prophets had spoken.

But would the Messiah, the Saviour, speak of giving His *flesh* to eat and His *blood* to drink when they offered to recognize Him, when they offered to proclaim Him king?

And was He not a man, even though He did such wonders? Did not everyone know that His father was a carpenter in nearby Nazareth, that His mother was right here with Him, in the company of some other relatives from His mountain village?

Jeremias spoke of a Saviour. They were expecting a Saviour, and one who would be linked somehow with the mystery of the Passover.* . . . the mystery of their delivery from Egypt. That is why this miracle of the bread and fish was significant. The Passover had been marked by a miraculous feeding after the miracle of seven plagues and the parting of the sea.

They said to Him when He promised bread which would enable them to live forever: "We want this Bread! We want this Bread!"

Each year the Jews relived the Pasch, or Passover. Each year, following their ancient covenant* with God they girded themselves as for a trip as had their forefathers on that fateful night in Egypt. They slaughtered a lamb, marked the doorposts with the blood, and ate it in a ritual of brotherhood and prayer reminiscent of that night when God showed a final sign to convince the Pharaoh of Egypt to set them free. On that night an angel of death struck down the firstborn in every house of Egypt, passing over those houses marked by the blood of the lamb.

Now this Christ, armed with the lightning of miracles and the gentleness of a lamb and the mystery of a prophet, speaks of giving his *own* blood.

How could this make Him their Saviour? They wanted freedom from Rome, and can drinking a man's blood bring freedom? They wanted power, and can eating a man's flesh give power?

There is one disquieting thought.

When they had been released from the clutches of Egypt, God had to work miracles constantly to preserve their freedom and their life. He had to destroy armies which the vacillating Pharaoh sent after them. He had to feed them in the desert . . . and for this was needed *a daily miracle* of mysterious bread which every day fell upon the sands in sufficient quantity. And that bread was adequate food.

So when Christ said that instead of becoming their King He would give them bread to eat which would prevent them from dying, they were not completely incredulous. Their forefathers had eaten manna in the desert.

But was it really possible that this was how they were to be saved, by bread? If so, would He give another sign so they could truly believe something so unbelievable?

Too bad. They would have to wait. They would have to believe something far more astounding than mere bread falling on desert sand. They would have to believe something so incredible that it would become the world's greatest secret, kept from all but the "initiated" for hundreds of years and still secret to millions right into the twentieth century, when men would still be gasping at the explanation of what He meant.

Understanding first began to dawn after all the prophecies concerning Christ had been fulfilled: the prophecies of Jeremias which described Him as a Man of Sorrows, of David who said of Him that "They have pierced my hands and my feet, they have numbered all my bones," of Isaias, Ezechiel, of Osse who cried "Where is thy King?" (13,10), and of Malachias who prophesied: "From the rising of the sun to the going down my name is great among the Gentiles and in every place there is a sacrifice . . . a clean oblation." (I,11)

In the early centuries Christians formulated this understanding in an act of faith known as the "Nicene Creed" which is still the profession of faith of most Christians in every part of the world today:

"For us men and for our salvation, He came down from heaven and was incarnate."

The new Pasch, or Passover, was to provide *a new and saving sacrifice* to revolutionize the world. It would turn the year of His birth into the year I.

It was to distill the good out of all the civilization of the past into a single chalice of incredible love which eventually would transform warring communities into a world governed by fraternal law.

For two years Christ did not explain the "hard saying." He did not destroy His enemies by saying to the people: "Come back, I'll tell you what it means and you can proclaim Me King." He gave even His own disciples nothing more than a clue: The secret was "Spirit and life."

Then came that last night of the Passover. He was finally ready to admit that He was indeed a King. But His kingdom was "not of this world." For the first time He proclaimed clearly that He was the Saviour: "For this was I born, for this did I come into the world." (John 18,37) Now He was about to explain the hard saying. Now He was about to explain what all the prophets had meant by the "salvation." And He began His whole extraordinary revelation with these words:

"I have greatly desired to eat this passover with you before I suffer." (Luke 22,15)

Never before had He "greatly desired" anything. He did not explain that within a few hours He would submit to imprisonment, mockery, scourging, and finally death by crucifixion. Now, *this moment of passover* was the moment for which He had longed. Everything else, all the teaching of the past years and all of His suffering of tomorrow, was contingent on this moment and this act He was about to perform and for which He had so ardently longed.

Now the purpose of His coming and of His thirty-three years on this earth was to be made clear. Now was the hour when He would explain what He had meant when He said that *He would enable men to live forever by eating His flesh and blood.* Now He would fulfill the old law by giving a new cove-nant* between God and man, a covenant sealed in one final bloodletting that would so far outweigh in value all the bloody sacrifices of the past that the world would be able henceforth to offer "In every place a clean oblation for My name is great among the Gentiles, said the Lord of Hosts." (Malachias, I,11)

In a few moments they would know that the relationship between God and man was no longer to be a secret of Israel, but was to be between God and all men. And this is how He began that eventful revelation in the year 33, the last night of His life:

Over their protests He washed their feet and said: *"A new commandment I give to you, That you love one another.* By this will all men know that you are my disciples, if you have love for one another." (John 13,31)

But where were they to find such love? He was not asking them merely to love each other person in the room, including the very one who in a few moments would betray them all. He was saying that *anyone* who was to be saved, anyone who wanted to follow Him, would have to love all men as brothers the way *He* loved them, unto death.

Now He told them openly that He was "ONE" with God: "When you see Me, you see the Father also." He explained a great deal about the very nature of God*: although of one nature, He was three persons. One Person (the Father) had sent Him; another Person (the Spirit) He would send so they would be able to understand all they had been taught; He himself was the "Son".

Philip, showing how much the Paraclete was needed even after three years of listening to Christ and even of seeing Him raise dead persons back to life, cried out:

"Lord, show us the Father and it is enough for us!"

He replied, perhaps with an air of frustrated weariness:

"Have I been so long a time with you and have you not known Me? Philip, he who sees Me also sees the Father. How can you say 'Show us the Father'? Do you not believe that I am in the Father and the Father in Me?"

Thus minute by minute, phrase by phrase, He led them toward that dramatic, climactic moment of the second most historic passover in history . . . the moment of the world's greatest secret.

Now He was to reveal the mystery of men eating His flesh and blood. Now He was to reveal how He was Himself to become the ultimate Lamb of Sacrifice, the salvation of the world. Now a new passover was to begin of which the old was merely symbolic. Now men were to pass from the slavery of materialism to the freedom of children of God. Now, with the intervention of God "fighting for them" (Exodus, 14,14) men would have the daily aid of a miracle greater than manna in the desert. It would be a bread which would enable them to live *forever*. Their passage would not be merely from physical bondage to another land, but from spiritual bondage to freedom of the spirit. They would become one with the Father by becoming one with Him, and thus all men might eventually be one: "As you and I are one " He prayed for them to the Father as He proceeded to the great moment for which He had so long desired.

Saint Matthew (26,26) describes what followed in these words:

"And while they were at supper Jesus took bread, and blessed and broke it and gave it to His disciples saying: *'Take and eat, this is My body.'*

"And taking a cup, He gave thanks and gave it to them saying, 'All of you drink of this, for *this is My blood* of the new covenant *which is being shed for many unto the forgiveness of sins."*

Now they understood! "Behold, now Thou speakest plainly!" one of them cried aloud. Saint

John describes the disciples exclaiming: "Now we know . . . For this reason we believe Thou camest forth from God." (John 16,30)

But did they know, really? Or did they recognize only that He was one with the Father, and they would become one with the Father by becoming one with Him by perpetuating this miracle by which He had just transformed an ordinary passover sacrifice into the world's first Eucharistic liturgy*?

There was too much for them to understand without further supernatural aid. First He would have to go through the passion to show the extent of the love of which He spoke. Next He would have to prove it all again by performing His greatest miracle, His own resurrection. Finally He would instruct them further, then send the Paraclete who "will teach you all the truth." (John 16,13)

Then would fall a great curtain of secrecy.

The Gospels themselves would be written in terms which would in general be understood only by the initiated, by those trusted, instructed, baptized and confirmed. The world at large would not know.

Years of persecution would deepen the secrecy. The ritual of that historic passover would be called "The Secret" until the twentieth century and Vatican Council II, when excavations in Rome were confirming what some had never dared explain to an unprepared world.

CHAPTER V

DISCOVERY

GUARDED IN THE CAVES of Palestine and in the subterranean cemeteries of Rome, the sacred rite of the
Blessed Sacrament, which made Christians literally
blood brothers, has been found hidden in symbols.
Paul said it made them "Of one body, all partaking
of one bread." But who, except the initiated, could
know the meaning of these powerful words let alone
the symbols of them?

Thus excavations unearthing Peter's tomb revealed rarities much more intriguing than the scrib-
blings of ancient pilgrims. Experts who had been
studying such enigmas throughout the Mediterranean
area from Athens to Rome, from Alexandria to Palestine, worked impatiently to decipher the findings:
effort at cover-up. But tradition, or word-of-mouth
knowledge held tightly and passed on intact through
all the centuries, provided some guidelines even as
it had provided the initial bit of knowledge that

Most of the symbols found around the tomb of Peter are difficult to see in a photograph. Some are clearer but still require interpretation by experts. Notice the meaningful additions to the Cross in the inscription here, with symbols of Eucharist and Christ.

Peter was buried on the spot where they found his tomb.

One particular symbol baffled them, although it had been showing up in excavation after excavation for a hundred and fifty years. It usually appeared on tombs, and usually, too, next to the symbol for Christ. Also it appeared on rings, domestic objects and it was often impressed on Roman documents of the fourth and fifth centuries. It was at last proven to be the symbol for Peter.

Dr. M .Guarducci writes[1]: "With the discovery of the symbol's meaning we now have an idea of the immense popularity enjoyed by Peter during the early centuries of Christianity . . ."

Also it would seem to indicate his importance in the minds of Christians as their spiritual leader, and as the first purely human head of the Church. It was so commonly used that it eventually became the symbol for Rome itself. It was found on an epigraph commemorating the restoration of the Colosseum and on metal coins found throughout the Roman world after the first centuries.

Popular though this symbol was, it was less popular than some others, especially those in the other catacombs. Recurring over and over again with more frequency than any others are the *symbols*

[1] THE TOMB OF ST. PETER, Hawthorne, April 1960, p.109.

Some of the inscriptions spoke of Mary and Christ, together with Peter, but above all they bore witness to a great secrecy.

*of Christ, Mary, and above all, the Eucharist.**

One symbol for Christ was an X (first letter of "Christos" in Greek) or an X with a T through its center. The symbol for Mary was sometimes just a simple M, sometimes an M on which an A was superimposed. Paradoxically, this second symbol for Mary was not only clearer to the initiated, but it was less clear to the outsider.

Symbols for the Eucharist were multiple: a fish; loaves surmounted by a fish; a bunch of grapes or a vine; a cup often resembling a large vase.

These symbols found around Peter's tomb make his burial place different from most found in the catacombs. The other tombs bear engravings or "graffiti" dealing with death and salvation. The graffiti on Peter's tomb, like those on the walls surrounding an altar table and on the walls of the underground passages and rooms, were hiding something as well as telling something, and here it was that the symbol of the Eucharist dominated. Obviously the Eucharist was the treasure prized and reverenced by Peter and his contemporaries, and it was the *sine qua non* of their religious rites.

Substantiating the cryptography and symbols are many pictures recently found in the catacombs. Cryptography is for experts. Pictures are for everybody, or at least for everybody who has ever been exposed to Christianity's secret. Naturally the ancient pagans

Sometimes early Christians showed the fish surmounted by a basket of bread, as here in the crypt of Lucina, in the Catacombs of St. Callixtus. Note the glass of wine in the midst of the bread.

A fresco from about the year 190 in the Catacombs of St. Callixtus.

There is something joyful about this scene although in a sad place: a subterranean chapel where hundreds of cruelly martyred Christians have been buried. Why a banquet with nothing but bread?

And why twelve enormous baskets of bread for seven persons? The latter recall that: "They filled twelve baskets with the fragments." And the number of seven symbolized the Church.

would not have understood even the pictures. What
pagan would suspect that a cup of wine and a loaf
of bread, the most ordinary and basic of foodstuffs,
signified a religious mystery* as deep as the one proclaimed by Christ on that hill by Capharnaum?
What pagan would ever suspect that a fish served
with a few loaves of bread signified a great miracle*;
or that a vine symbolized the heart of Christian ritual; or that a woman holding a child with the sun
behind her signified the coming of God to His earth
as man?

These are the very pictures recently found not
only near Peter's tomb but in the miles and miles
of catacombs* being dug out in our own day under
and around the walls of Rome.

One well-preserved fresco was painted within
the lifetime of persons directly instructed by Peter
and Paul. It was found in the catacomb of the famous Roman martyr Priscilla who is mentioned by St.
Paul in his second epistle to Timothy.

Like most of the other pictures from apostolic
times, it does not depict baptism or the resurrection,
nor a message about faith and good works. It shows
seven people reclining at table, eating bread and
drinking wine (see next page).

The number seven, as we know, is a favorite
one in the Bible and it stands for an uncertain
quantity. The same number of people, seven, are

Fresco in the Catacomb of St. Priscilla

found in several other "Supper-of-the-Lord" scenes elsewhere in the catacombs.

In this particular picture in the catacomb of St. Priscilla one of the seven persons is a woman. In the place of honor is the person who is breaking the bread. In front of Him on a table is a single, two-handled cup.

A fresco painted about the year 190 was found in another catacomb, St. Calixtus'. Again there are seven banqueters breaking bread, but what would appear unusual in this picture, perhaps even to the pagan, are twelve immense baskets in the foreground, standing higher than the table and filled to overflowing with bread.

There is something very joyful about this scene. It is in a subterranean chapel where the pitiful remains of hundreds of martyred Christians have been gathered from the debris of the arena. Yet the aspect of the primitive figures in the fading fresco is of a group celebrating at a great banquet. Now the pagan might well ask, what kind of banquet is this where the guests seem to be eating only bread and have but one cup of wine for all?

Elsewhere in the catacombs the bread is shown with incisions in the form of a cross. One picture found in a catacomb near the Via Appia Antica shows a much more complete account of the Eucharist in a threefold image. In the center Christ is performing the miracle of the multiplication. Then He is shown in the right with His hand raised in a gesture of blessing or thanks or of speech-making, while in the folds of His cloak are five loaves marked with a cross. On the left section of the picture is shown the Samaritan woman drawing water from Jacob's well, the woman to whom Christ promised to give "living water".

Any Christian can understand the picture. The center panel, of the prefiguring miracle, proved Christ's claim to be God, and so it also proved that He could do the humanly impossible: give Himself as food to His followers. The bread marked with a cross depicted the "holy bread" of His Eucharistic Body by which He did in fact give Himself to His followers; and the raised hand is a gesture of blessing as He speaks the words of transubstantiation. Finally, the Samaritan woman who was an adulterous sinner when she first met Christ could, because she repented, receive from Him the "living water" which is "for the remission of sins".

Few of the early Christian murals contain, as this one does, three sections. In fact, the most commonly seen picture is very simple: it is that of a fish. Sometimes the fish is surmounted by a basket of bread, and sometimes also a glass of red wine is depicted inside the basket and both bread and wine stand over a fish.

The fish has a double significance. Obviously

In the catacombs of Saint Priscilla (who was known by Saint Paul) archeologists found these sculpted loaves incised with a cross attached to a tomb. They recall the hope of Christians: "If anybody eats this bread he will live forever."

it represents the miracle of the multiplication as well as the "food from heaven" which Christ promised the next day, the food which was Himself, His body and blood. Also the letters of the Greek word for fish, icthys, are the initial letters in that language for "Jesus Son of God and Saviour" (Jesous Christos Theou Uios Soter).

This most famous acrostic* of the early Christian era interchangeably symbolized Christians, Christ Himself, and Christ in the Sacrament of the Eucharist through which Christians and Christ unite in a special way.

The epitaph of Bishop Abercius of Hieropolis in Phrygia can serve as a sort of synopsis of the Christian secret. He went to Rome about ninety years after St. Peter's death, at a time when the persecutions had already taken heavy toll although the worst was yet to come.

The authenticity of his ancient epitaph was confirmed by the findings of an English traveler named Ramsey, who found an inscribed slab in Phrygia dated 216 A.D., which verified the older text of the epitaph of Abercius. The significance of the words was recognized by scholars. Later research revealed continued fragments of the same epitaph which had been built into the walls of the public baths in Phrygia. They filled out the complete message which Abercius, for the benefit of posterity, had ordered cut into the stone which was to go above

This fresco found in one of the catacombs (Saints Peter and Marcellinus) shows Christ multiplying bread. It was made about the year 200. In all the catacombs there have been so many discoveries of such symbolic pictures that the photographs fill many albums in the Vatican archives. The archivist at the Catacomb of Saint Priscilla notes that the frequency of subjects in these early Christian symbols and pictures is: First) Multiplication of loaves and fishes; Second) The "Breaking of Bread" or the Eucharistic Banquet; Third) Various other miracles of Jesus.

his tomb. (Leclercq: Dict. d'Archeol. Chrét. et de Liturgie,I,66-87)

The message begins: *"Let the brother who shall understand* pray for Abercius." Thus announcing that he was about to record Christian secrets in a manner only Christians could understand, he writes:

"I am by name Abercius, disciple of the Holy Shepherd[1] Who feeds flocks of sheep on the mountains and plains, Who has great eyes[2] that see everywhere. This Shepherd taught me that the book of life is worthy of belief. And to Rome He sent me to contemplate Majesty and to see a Queen, golden-robed and golden-sandaled[3]; there also I saw people bearing a shining mark."[4] Later he continues:

"Faith everywhere led me forward and everywhere provided as my food a fish[5] of exceeding great size and perfection which a Holy Virgin drew with her hands from a fountain and ever gives this to its friends to eat, wine of great virtue, mingled with bread."

Scholars declare that a mystic or a theologian of today might have difficulty in expressing so much of the doctrine of the Eucharist in so few words,

---

[1] Christ was particularly identified by early Christians as the "Good Shepherd."
[2] The all-seeing eye is both a symbol and a definition of God. Thus he here asserts that Christ is God.
[3] The Church.
[4] Baptism which dogma says confers an "indelible mark".
[5] Symbol meaning **Jesus Christ Son of God Saviour.**

though it might be expressed in less veiled terms. Without secrecy the words could read: Faith showed me that everywhere I went I received Jesus Christ, Son of God and Saviour, to whom the holy virgin Mary had given flesh and blood, and now gives Him to me in the form of wine of great virtue served with bread.

"These writings," the epitaph concludes, "I, Abercius, having been a witness thereto, have told to be written here. Verily, I am passing through my seventy-second year."

If Abercius' epitaph seems a little abstruse or even far-fetched to those of us who are neither scholars nor archeological experts, we can turn to other inscriptions. They are legion. In one of the catacombs is found an inscription written by Pope Damasus on the tomb of a young man who was killed while carrying Eucharistic bread. He refused to reveal to those who stopped him what it was he had on his person. His name was Tarcisius and his feast day is kept by the Church on July seventeenth. The inscription on his tomb reads: "Carrying the Sacrament of Christ, he chose rather to suffer death than to betray the heavenly Body to the raging dogs."

Tradition tells us that he was only a boy and that a pagan mob, alerted to the fact that he was carrying the "secret" of the Christians to a co-religionist, tortured him to know what it was. Since they found only "bread" on his person, the boy preferred

to die letting them think it was mere bread rather
than risk desecration of the Eucharist as the real
Body of Christ.

Ours is a blessed age in which these facts of
early Christianity are finally brought to light. They
reveal what was once considered the secret of secrets,
the transcendent Eucharistic doctrine. Together
with the infusion of the Holy Spirit, this was the
life principle of the Christian Church, or the Mystical Body of Christ, by which Christians "may be
made one" as the Saviour said to His Father: "As
You and I are One."

But even as the world in general was not prepared to grasp such a secret after the miracle of the
loaves and fishes, would the world be ready to grasp
it when the secret began to leak into general knowledge? To what extent would it remain secret even
down to the twentieth century, when finally Vatican
Council II would remove the word "Secret"?

Chapter VI

THE SECRET, GOSPEL TRUTH

It is little wonder that the fish (meaning Jesus Christ, Son of God, Saviour) was frescoed into the catacomb walls surmounted by loaves and wine.

When we turn from the discoveries and archeology to reread the Gospels, we find something we may never really have seen before: *that it was the Eucharist which Christ Himself emphasized.* Not only did He make It the test of faith at Capharnaum, but at the eleventh hour, on the very eve of His death, He held It up to His followers as His legacy and His pledge of His ever-abiding Presence. At this time, when He knew that these, His last acts and words, would be cherished and remembered more vividly than any which had gone before, what did He do and say?

Though He spoke of love, He did not try to summarize His sermons and His parables. He did not remind His apostles of past miracles or favors. He did not exhort His followers to live up to His precepts nor extract any promises of fidelity from them. Instead, He gave them the Eucharist.

What is more, even though He would die a ter-

73

rible death in less than twenty-four hours, He identified the institution of the Eucharist with the passover and with the purpose of His coming. And never
before had He said that He ardently desired "this
moment," the moment when the secret of the miracle
of the loaves and fishes was finally revealed.

Immediately after Christ died in the short interval before Peter went to Rome, in the interval during which he and all the apostles remained in Jerusalem, we see that the Eucharist was already considered a sort of trademark for Christ and His followers.
It appears in the twenty-fourth chapter of St. Luke's
Gospel.

Two disciples of the Lord, Cleophas and his companion, were traveling about seven or eight miles from
Jerusalem to Emmaus. Christ had been dead but
a scant three days and as they walked along the
dusty road they could talk of nothing else. The terrible, crushing grief which filled their minds and
hearts overflowed into words which eddied round
and round in repetition as they asked one another
time and again: "Were we fooled about this Jesus?
Was He really the Christ? Or was the fellow no more
than a rabble rouser seeking to stir up a to-do for
his own selfish ends? Or at best was He a good man
who was deluded, and so deluded others?"[1]

[1] Most Scriptural quotations are from the modern translations,
according to the author's own choice, especially from the
translations of Kiest-Lilly, Ronald Knox, The Oxford Bible, and
the Confraternity Version.

They shook their heads wearily and the one named Cleophas remarked: "It's beyond all understanding. I know only that all the light has gone out of my life. I feel that a part of me has died with Him."

His companion, whom the Gospel does not name, sighed: "Yes, what have we to hope for now? I wish . . ." He broke off abruptly. 'Here comes another traveler along the road."

The newcomer had scarcely greeted them when he noticed their downcast faces and their dejected air.

"What are you talking about? What makes you so sad?" He asked.

"Man, You ask that?" Cleophas exploded. "Are you a stranger in Jerusalem that you don't know what has happened there these past few days?"

"What has happened?" the newcomer asked.

With one voice the two travelers answered: "Jesus of Nazareth is dead . . . crucified as a common criminal."

But the unnamed one went on: "This Jesus of Nazareth was a prophet, mighty in work and word before God, and before all the people. Our high priests and the princes of the realm delivered Him to be condemned to death, and they nailed Him to the tree."

"But we hoped that it would be He Who would redeem Israel. We hoped that He was the Christ, the Messiah," Cleophas explained.

"And besides all this," Cleophas' companion took up, "this is the third day since His death, and certain women of our group have been saying strange things. Before the light came out of the east, early in the morning, they went to His sepulchre and they did not find His body. They said that they saw an angel who told them that He is alive. What are we to think?"

"And others besides the women went to the sepulchre and found it just as the women said. His body was gone," Cleophas added quickly.

As their words tumbled out the newcomer traveler listened intently. It was only when they came to pause at last that He answered them: "You are really slow to see and to believe what the prophets have written. Shouldn't Christ have suffered these things and entered into His glory?"

With that as a prelude, the "stranger" began to talk of the prophecies in the Scriptures. Tracing them all the way back to Moses, He showed how the texts foretold for the Saviour of the world just such a rejection by His people and death at their hands.

Cleophas and his companion were silent. Their dark eyes were riveted on the speaker as they drank in His every word. It was all so logical and so convincing, and the stranger was so eloquent and so compelling. They paid no attention to the passing of time as He talked until they suddenly spied from

the crest of the hill the squat building of the inn lying
in the valley below. It was there that they had
planned to stop for the last meal of the day and to
rest.

When they mentioned this to the stranger, He
murmured something about going on farther Himself.

"Oh no!" the other two protested. "It is late
now. Stop with us."

Obviously they were extremely reluctant to
part company and their persuasion soon won over
their chance fellow traveler. He entered the inn
with them.

A little later the three men sat at a table
and the stranger picked up the bread set before
them, held it for a moment in His strong, sun-tanned
hands, blessed it, broke it and gave it to them.

Scarcely had the two disciples of Christ swal-
lowed the morsel when they both sprang to their feet
as though propelled by some outside force. This
man was no longer a stranger! He was . . . "Oh
Lord," they cried, and thrust out their arms as
though to clutch Him, but He vanished from their
sight.

"Ah, it was He!" breathed Cleophas. "Wasn't
your heart burning within you when He spoke . . .
when He explained the Scriptures?"

"Yes, it was He!"

"But we can't sit here," Cleophas said, wrapping his cloak about him and turning toward the door. "We must go back to Jerusalem. We must tell Peter and the others."

Forthwith, leaving their frugal meal upon the table, they rushed out into the gathering dusk and retraced their steps to Jerusalem, back to the place where the eleven apostles were hiding. Bursting in upon the little gathering they all but shouted: "We have seen the Lord! It was He and no mistake about it. *We knew Him in the breaking of the bread.*"

After the story of the travelers on their way to Emmaus, other references to the Eucharist appear in the Bible although almost with an air of secrecy.

St. Paul, in Chapter 11 of his first epistle to the Corinthians, writes of the Last Supper saying: ". . . the same night that He was betrayed (He) took bread. And giving thanks, broke, and said, 'Take this and eat it. This is my body which shall be delivered for you. Do this in commemoration of me.' In like manner also the chalice, after He had supped saying, 'This chalice is the new testament of my blood. This do as often as you shall drink for a commemoration of me. For as often as you shall eat this bread and drink this chalice you shall show the death of the Lord until He comes.

"Therefore, whoever shall eat this bread, or drink this chalice of the Lord unworthily shall be guilty of the body and blood of the Lord.

"But let a man prove himself; and so let him

eat of that bread and drink of that chalice. For he that eateth and drinketh unworthily, eateth and drinketh judgment to himself, not discerning the body of the Lord."

St. Luke writes in the second chapter of the Acts of the Apostles (Verse 42): "And they were persevering in the doctrine of the apostles, and in the communication of the breaking of the bread . . ." Then in the same chapter (Verse 46) he speaks of them "breaking bread from house to house," indicating that this was the usual procedure when Christians gathered together. Also in the Acts of the Apostles, (Chapter XX, 7) we read: "And on the first day of the week, when we were assembled to break bread . . ."

For years after early apostolic days, fear tied the hands of the Christian scribes and scholars, so that little was written about the Eucharist, or for that matter about any aspect of the Faith. However, knowledge of the Eucharistic Doctrine and practice of the Eucharistic Liturgy were passed along from generation to generation by what we call "tradition". Happily, tradition is reliable. It is akin to Gospel truth.

It would have to be. No ordinary mortal would come equipped with the inventiveness necessary to make up a story like the Eucharistic one. Or, if some strange being did invent it, no ordinary mortal would perpetuate it. For such an idea to have originated and to have endured, it would have to be more certain than surmise in the minds of Christians. They were willing to die for it. Moreover it was not a tenet calculated to recruit new members to the struggling, infant church. On the contrary! It was a tenet which would repel most people; they would consider it too fantastic for belief and an insult to their common sense. Nevertheless the little band of Christians stuck to it and passed it on to their children, and their children to their children, through the years. And they did die for it.

It was tradition* alone which held together the chain of teaching in unbroken sequence through the years of persecution and secrecy. As a matter of fact comparatively few people in pagan Rome could read. The Gospels and the whole collection of sacred writings that we now call the Bible were not assembled and compiled into one book until after the periods of the persecution. The Deposit of Faith then, was handed down orally from one Christian to another for almost four centuries until the Bible was compiled and until other manuscripts and books of all sorts could publicly record it.

Today, thanks to the ever-advancing science of archeology, we are beginning to find evidence which corroborates the writings as well as the tradition. But we may never find corroboration of all details. Nor have the writings themselves recorded every detail. We still must look to tradition to flesh out the skeleton of the written word which wasn't filled out until after the time of secrecy.

Recently at a luncheon meeting of some prominent men somebody asked: "How did Lincoln pronounce those words of his address '. . . of the people, by the people, for the people'?"

All answered: ". . . *of* the people, *by* the people, *for* the people."

But one person added: "Actually I suppose we can never know for sure. *It has never been recorded.*"

"Anything about the address is important," remarked another man who happened to be Naval Attache to the United States Embassy in Rome, "for it is the epitome of the American doctrine, and certainly one of the most significant documents of all time."

Then the writer of this book who had first broached the subject said: "Lincoln stressed '. . . a government of the *people,* by the *people,* and for the *people.*' My English teacher was corrected on this point by his teacher *who heard Lincoln say it.*"

Perhaps no one ever thought to record Lincoln's inflection in these past one hundred years. Our grandparents or our great-grandparents knew many, many persons who were contemporaries of Lincoln. They had not appreciated the importance of the Address at Gettysburg when it was delivered. It was but a small fragment from a war which marked a black and baneful passage in their lives.

Yet any one of hundreds could have written a note to correct the countless school children who emphasized the wrong words. Apparently nobody ever bothered to write it . . . until now, a hundred years later, here in this book.

So it must have been with early Christianity. Only tradition saves some small facts. Because of secrecy caused by persecution only tradition saved even important facts until the day when, comparatively free of persecution, the so-called "Fathers and Doctors of the Church"* could record them in writing. In the fourth century these hardy souls began to defend Christ's teaching against the objections of the non-Christian world and to put Christian teaching down in legible black and white.

Though one "Father" wrote in Africa, another in Athens, another in what is now Istanbul, another in Rome, *they were all found to agree in their teachings and writings*. This is another proof (if we need it) for the validity of the tradition they recorded.

What these first writers (now called Fathers of the Church*) taught about the Eucharist is just as amazing and just as "unbelievable" as what Christ Himself (according to the Gospel account) told the crowd which turned away from Him in Capharnaum. It was an explanation after three hundred years of experience.

CHAPTER VII

SCIENCE AND THE SECRET

IN THE INTRODUCTION to this book we mentioned that four thousand copies of an advance edition were used for a survey to test whether or not the book held interest throughout and, if not, where interest lagged. Many said they found this one chapter "difficult."

By contrast, a Teilhard de Chardin enthusiast answered that this chapter was "the high point of the book."

So we did two things: 1) We tried to make it easier to read; 2) We asked one of the nation's top experts on the atom, Dr. Francis J. Heyden*, to give his advice.

The world's greatest secret would be better left secret if it were to appear as ridiculous to many in the modern world as it appeared when Christ first announced it in Capharnaum, causing thousands who had previously hung on His every word to be repulsed and to turn away. How, for example, will those millions behind the Iron Curtain, who know a great deal of science and little about Christ, react to this central secret of Christianity?

To the believer, no explanation is necessary. To the non-believer, a great deal of explanation is now possible.

First, let us remember that even after fifteen hundred years the impact of Christ's miracles was so great that *all* Christians believed in the Eucharist. Even Martin Luther*, who set in motion the world's first wave of disbelief, himself believed. In *Wider Etliche Tollen Geister,* 1532, he testified that "the whole of Christendom accepts the doctrine of the Real Presence*. In *This is My Body,* published in 1527, he wrote: "These words of Christ still stand firm against the fanatics." (See LUTHER, pg. 296)

So it must be evident to any intelligent person that apparently the Eucharist is really credible because millions upon millions of persons . . . indeed those who have given us most of our present culture . . . almost *unanimously* believed it. And there were even geniuses among them.

It is evident that they believed primarily because, as one of the greatest intellects of the middle ages concluded: "Christ told us so"

After the Fathers of the Church* had explained it, one man named Paschasius Radbertus questioned it in the 9th century but never got a following. Then a man named Berengarius, of Tours, raised a question which gave the Church its first occasion to defend the belief in a dramatic, official manner. Berengarius made a sincere retraction at a synod held in Rome in 1079, and so it was not until the time of Martin Luther, that is until almost our own day, that this early secret of Christians became a basis of division.

Now, for the first time, the Church found it necessary to *define* the belief.

So the Bishops of the world were convened in Trent*, less than twenty-five years after Luther nailed his theses on the door of a church in Wittemberg. What they proclaimed was almost taken verbatim from the Fathers of the Church:

"Jesus Christ, our God and Saviour, although He offered Himself once and for all to God the Father on the altar of the cross by His death, there to work out our eternal redemption, yet (since His priesthood was not to end with His death) He left to His Church at the Last Supper a visible sacrifice. This sacrifice, the Eucharist, was what our nature required. The Eucharist presents the Sacrifice of Christ to the Father, once and for all wrought upon the cross. Through the Eucharist, the memory of the cross will abide to the end of the world. Moreover, its saving power of grace will be applied for the remission of those sins that we all fall into day by day. Declaring Himself to be a priest forever 'according to the Order of Melchisedech' Christ of-

fered His body and blood to God the Father under
the appearance of bread and wine, and gave them
under the same appearance to His apostles. He then
made these men and their successors priests of the
New Testament by the words, 'Do this in commemoration of me.' So Christ gave the command to offer
the Eucharist as the Church has always understood
and taught."

The Council of Trent document, written in
1545, then went on to say that even as the Christian
community consists of many Church members, "of
this union nothing is more strikingly illustrative than
the elements of bread and wine, for bread is made
from grains of wheat and wine is pressed from many
clusters of grapes. Thus they signify that we, though
many, are closely bound together by a bond of this
divine mystery and made, as it were, one body."

Unbelievable! Thus do many Christians exclaim
after reading this definition of the Eucharist formulated at Trent. It is not borne out by our senses. We
moderns who fancy ourselves scientific shy away
from anything which cannot be put into a test tube
and proved by laboratory experiment.

We look at what we call the Host. It seems
to be a bit of white bread of cracker-like consistency.
Is that Christ?

Isn't the whole idea incredible, not to say
absurd?

This is where modern science comes to our aid.

Now, with some understanding of the *nature of matter,* the miracle of the Eucharist (aside from the greater mystery of the Incarnation and considering only the fact of transubstantiation*) appears plausible. This does not mean that reason alone, aided by science, can *explain* it. But it means that much of the mystery as to *how* transubstantiation takes place is stripped away.

Especially for those who may find the following explanation a little difficult, we cannot overstress the fact that ultimately one pierces through the mystery of the Eucharist only with the force of faith.

If we could understand the mysteries of God, we would be no longer merely human; we would be what our first parents wished to be: as gods.

One is reminded of the tale told of the great "Doctor" Augustine who wanted to write about the Trinity* and of course met great difficulty in finding words for such ineffable truth. The more he thought the more baffled he became.

One day as he was walking along the seashore pondering his problem he saw a little boy playing in the sand. The child was digging a hole and pouring water into it from a tin pail. To give himself a brief respite from his vexing thoughts, the theologian stopped to speak to the child. He asked: "What are you doing, lad?"

The boy answered: "I am going to empty the whole ocean into this hole."

Augustine suddenly realized that it was no more ridiculous for the child to be trying to pour the ocean into a hole than it was for him to be trying to pour understanding of the Infinite into his human brain.

While acknowledging our inability to explain the inexplicable, we can consider some of the findings of modern science which may have a tangential relationship to the Eucharist. If we can understand matter itself we can perhaps understand how the Eucharistic miracle happens.

To the modern scientist, matter is nothing more than plain energy. It is as though positive electricity and negative electricity were counterbalanced to give quantity to substance.*

This is not difficult to understand. Atomic energy has been harnessed as the direct result of this hypothesis which is now taught as a matter of course to most school children.

Even before the atom bomb this hypothesis was held by many scientists. Twenty-five years before writing this book (that is a few years before the atom bomb) the author presumed to write in another book:[2] What makes a table or a wall or a stone *resist* pressure? We believe it to be nothing more than positive points of *force*, held in place by correlative negative points of force. Electricity has not

[1] FROM A MORNING PRAYER, 275pp First published 1942. Later edition AMI Press 1960.

quantity because it is merely points of force in the pure positive or negative state. And the proof that something *without* quantity could *constitute* quantity is found in the fact that a bolt of lightning can split a giant tree as though it were a mighty steel ax.

Naturally, between a positive point of force and a negative point of force there is an electrical *field*. Since all the world is fundamentally constituted of these positive and negative points of force, this field is universal. The undulations of this field constitute light and sound. Some undulations pass through most densities of the universal field, but there are certain densities through which they cannot pass. For example, light passes through the field that exists between the planets, but it is 'undone', as it were, by the field in a piece of wood. Radio can transmit light and sounds by reducing them to a strange undulation that is not undone by most fields, and then reproducing and undoing the original undulations in a receiving set.

"We would imagine that the five senses work similarly. It is not an electrical impulse that rushes to the brain when a man sees something. The optic nerve is merely a receiving set, undoing the undulation of light to which it is sensitive and reducing it to a new undulation: the type of undulation to which the sense of touch reduces tactile sensation . . . the same undulation to which the ear reduces sound . . . the same undulation that causes all things sensed by man to seem *one* sensation and to be thus the tool of his active intelligence."

So it would appear, from the apparent confirmation of this theory by radio, television, X-ray, and finally atomic power, that matter is indeed merely *forces* in juxtaposition.

This suddenly opens a possibility of understanding the mode of the Eucharist. Before this men had to accept only on blind faith that the Body of Christ . . . without changing, and remaining entire . . . became contained in a tiny space and under new appearance. They had to believe only because Christ told them so (confirmed by miracles). Now we can accept the possibility that the *effect* of the forces of Christ's body merely become *suspended* with relation to the forces of a piece of bread.

Essentially this is not much different than the miracle witnessed by hundreds of reliable persons during one of the apparitions of the Virgin to Saint Bernadette: the saint's hand strayed into the flame of a lighted candle during her ecstacy, but did not burn. After the ecstacy a doctor reached the flame again to her hand. She cried out.

It is logical to conclude that her hand did not cease to be a hand, and the fire did not cease to be fire. But the *effect* of the fire was *suspended* with relation to Bernadette's hand during the ecstacy.

Similarly we may presume that the effect of the "matter" or body of Christ . . . which scientific experience tells us may be pure force . . . is suspended with relation to the absolute accidents* of bread and wine.

Can we state positively that Christ's physical presence under the appearance of bread and wine would mean that *the points of force in His physical quantity* were present but *their effect was withheld by divine power?*

We can say this much: The energy concept of matter is accepted today as a working fact, and that seems to make the mystery of the Eucharist, though still supernatural and miraculous, not quite so covered with misty clouds.

Indeed, in the pre-Einstein era, when the energy concept of matter was still no more than an exciting but much shakier hypothesis, Dr. J. Pohle, the celebrated professor of the University of Breslau, Germany, wrote in his book LEHRBUCH DER DOGMATIK: "Assuming a real distinction between force and its manifestations, between energy and its effects, it may be seen that under the influence of the first Cause, *the energy necessary for the essence of bread is withdrawn by the virtue of conversion, while the effects of the energy (accidents) in a miraculous manner continue.*" (C.E.Vol.V p.582)

Conversely, according to Pohle, when Christ becomes present in the Eucharist it is merely the *effects* of His physical energy (impenetrability, visibility) which are suspended. This explanation, at least in the opinion of some, adequately explains away the most apparent contradiction of the whole Christ . . . in the fulness of His manhood and of all His human and divine faculties . . . contained in such small space. If the *effect* of "points of force" of any body could be suspended, *the body could be contained in almost inconceivably small space.*

This is what our new discoveries about matter must lead us to believe.

Even long before help from modern science, geniuses of the Middle Ages began to shed great light upon the Christian "Secret" through the development of rational philosophy. Even some early Greek philosophers (as though anticipating the discovery that matter might be energy) drew a fine distinction between "modal" and "absolute accidents". Modal accidents were those which could not be separated from their substance without involving a metaphysical contradiction, like the form and motion of a body. On the other hand, absolute accidents were those accidents which could be separated from substance without involving metaphysical contradiction. Size (quantity of a body) they considered an absolute accident.

Aristotle, one of the greatest pre-Christian philosophers, taught essentially this. He defined substance as the *heart* of matter; accidents as the *modifications* of matter.

Einstein, whose theories contributed greatly to the discovery of atomic power, was afraid the explosion of even one bomb would set off a chain reaction which would cause all the earth's quantity to disintegrate, since matter is now believed to be nothing but energy. This very understanding of matter perhaps sheds light on Christianity's greatest secret . . . and deepest mystery.

The accidents of the Eucharist are bread whiteness, bread taste and bread size; the substance is
Christ. The physical reality of the whiteness, of the
taste and of the size of the Eucharist cannot be questioned. In other words, philosophers could reason
that Christ does not destroy the accidents of the bread
and replace it with a mirage suddenly created at the
moment of transubstantiation.

Aristotle also taught that quantity is not a corporal substance, but only a phenomenon of substance.
(METAPHYSICS VI, 3rd ed. of Boker,p1029,a.13)

This is precisely what scientists are trying to
prove today in using the working hypothesis that
matter is merely contained energy.

However, despite new evidence from centuries
of thought and discovery, matter (or substance) is
especially difficult to understand when it becomes
alive, and for many is understandable only on the
basis of authority and supernatural providence.

What, for example, causes a tiny speck in a
woman's womb to grow into a being so complex that
we produce more scientific books on this one subject
than on any other, and still have not scratched the
surface of understanding? What is that "something"
contained in a uterine speck so small that it is invisible to the naked eye, yet it multiplies millions of
times to the complexity of man?

We give it a name. We often call it entelechy.*
Yet giving it a name does not help us to understand

all that follows the moment of conception: an intricate unfolding of modifications of energy to fill out the "substance" of man.

In any event, when we realize that a man is potentially contained in a tiny cell, it no longer seems quite so difficult to believe that Christ could be wholly, substantially present in a wafer consecrated for us to consume.

Yet if He had not told them so, if they had not heard it from His lips or read His own words in the Bible, and if the testimony of two thousands years of Christian experience did not confirm it, how could Christians ever believe it?

Faith alone conquers all objections like that of the little girl in the story. Her father gave her a crucifix and asked: "What's the difference between the figure on the cross and the Host held up at the Consecration of the Mass?"

The child did not hesitate. She answered: "I look at the figure on the cross and I see Jesus, but He's not there. When I look at the Host, I don't see Jesus, but He *is* there."

We who lack the simple faith of children feel the need to know all we can because this secret of primitive Christianity is also a secret of life. So far its ultimate discovery by all Christians in the modern sweep of ecumenism must take us back to the words written by Christ's own disciples, Matthew, Mark, Luke and John.

Chapter VIII

BOOK OF THE SECRET

WE OFTEN SEE just a loaf of bread marked with a cross in the Mediterranean excavations.

Generation after generation of the ancient Jews told their children that the great one, the Messiah,* would be born in "the house of bread", or as the name is in Hebrew, Bethlehem.

"Where is He who is born king of the Jews?" was the question that was asked by certain foreigners newly arrived from the distant East. Following a strange star in the heavens they had traveled over misty mountains, through arid deserts, across broad valleys, until they came at last to Israel and to its capital city, Jerusalem.

The chief priests and the scribes there had an answer for the Easterners. The Holy Scriptures foretold that the expected of nations was to be born in the town known as "the house of bread".

From the moment that Christ lay like a kernel of wheat restored to the straw of the manger, one scene and one circumstance after another seems to tie in by symbolism and analogy with His future Eucharistic life. It was as though all His coming and all His days were directed, like the entelechy of living cells, toward the Eucharist.

Indeed, we can go back before His birth. At the moment of the Incarnation nine months before His birth we see a correlation between God-man in embryo* and God-man in bread. Surely His hiddenness in those nine months and His sanctification of John the Baptist suggest his hiddenness in the Eucharistic bread and his sanctification of all who approach Him there.[1] He might have been expected to materialize in some dazzling, glorious manner. But He chose to come as a speck of matter in a human tabernacle.

One could review His whole life as recorded in the Gospels and continue finding these connections and looking for this symbolism with marked success. His very first miracle, the one which inaugurated His public life, was the changing of the water into wine at the marriage feast of Cana. In the Eucharist He changes wine into His blood.

Let us try an experiment: Let us open the New Testament at random and by the spot-check method see how closely Christ's Palestinian life relates to His Eucharistic life.[2]

The first opening falls upon the tenth chapter of St. John. The first verse to meet our eyes reads:

[1] See PRESANCTIFICATION, page 302.

[2] This is an honest experiment. We will put on these pages whatever passages we find as we open the Bible.

"And they once again took up stones to stone Him with. Jesus answered them: *'Many good works have I showed you from My Father. For which of these works do you stone me?'*

" *'It is not for good works that we stone you,'* they answered. *'It is for blasphemy. You who are man, claim to be God.'* "

A few verses later we read: *"They sought therefore to take Him but He escaped out of their hands."*

Two facts strike us here: Christ claimed to be God, and at the moment of His choice He became invisible.

In this day of militant atheism stones still threaten Him in churches and in tabernacles where we assert His Divinity. But He constantly escapes and constantly renews His Presence. Just as He became invisible on the occasion of the Gospel story, so He becomes invisible now, hidden under the appearances of very ordinary looking bread. Heroic missionaries who consecrate the bread sometimes slip behind the Iron or the Bamboo Curtains *and no enemy detects the Lord Whom they bring with them.* He is both human and divine, yet He becomes invisible.

If you have a Bible at hand you might like to follow the experiment. This time the sacred book opens on Mark's tenth chapter. James and John have just asked Christ for a place on His right and left sides when He is glorified. He replies that they do not know what they are asking and He challenges:

"Can you drink of the cup I am to drink?"

Eagerly they say that they can. But He goes on to tell them that their request is not His to grant them, and He admonishes them for seeking so high a position. He says: *"Whoever has a mind to be great among you, must be your servant, and whoever has a mind to be first among you must be servant to all. For the Son of Man did not come to be ministered unto, but to minister . . ."*

How completely these words find fulfillment in the Eucharistic state of subjection. *He makes Himself dependent on men.*

Next our Bible falls open on the tenth chapter of St. Luke.

Here we find Christ in Bethany visiting the home of the sisters Mary and Martha. At the moment their brother Lazarus is out. Mary sits at the Master's feet listening to His words. Martha asks Christ to speak to Mary and bid her to help with the cooking. Christ answers: *"Martha, Martha, you are troubled about many things! But only one thing is necessary. Mary has chosen the best part."*

In this passage, again the dual nature of Christ is asserted, with emphasis on personal conversation with Him.

Where can we meet Christ in Person? Of course we can find God anywhere, wherever we happen to be at the moment, whether in a crowded subway, on a lonely mountain peak, in a bustling newspaper office, in a hospital bed. God is everywhere and we can always seek His Presence in prayer, in love and in the turning of our mind and heart to Him. He is at hand. Martha must have known and lived this truth and it is emphasized by many today who do not believe in the Eucharist.

But we can, according to the doctrine of the Eucharist, actually sit at His feet as Mary did in Bethany by walking to the nearest tabernacle.* The truth that He is everywhere is not always enough to evoke prayer. Even the truth that He dwells within our very souls is not always enough. It is sometimes too nebulous an idea for us to grasp solidly.

The secret of Christianity reveals that God had pity on us. He comes to our human weakness in human form as well as with His divinity. He comes in His own flesh and blood in the Eucharist. He is there in a set place, at a set time, *under the appearance of a visible and tangible thing* that we can see, and feel, and taste.

Patiently today He waits in the tabernacles throughout the world, hoping that a few Marys will stop to sit at His feet. Sadly today He addresses the millions upon millions of Marthas who, though they are good and just people, are so caught up in a whirlwind of activities and business that they rarely, if ever, find time for prayer in His Eucharistic Presence.

And He is so available! Could He have made Himself any more so than by entering thousands

4 5 1 b 9

upon thousands of tabernacles in every city and hamlet throughout the world?

If it might appear that some of our interpretations of the Bible passages we chose at random were contrived, let it be quickly admitted that many lessons can be drawn from the life of Christ. During the survey made before publication of this book, many tried the same experiment with varying success. Some came upon passages more apt than the three we quoted. But those passages in particular which assert His Divinity, His power of working miracles, and His desire for physical intimacy with us are obvious confirmations of the climactic events of the Last Supper. And what if we deliberately chose the passages from the Evangelists which we considered *appropriate* instead of opening the book at *random?*

Once we know the secret of Christianity, all that Christ did and said has new meaning. But even more, our present relationship with Him leaps to new life, wherever we may be in any corner of the world. That house in Bethany is no more honored than a place He has chosen in my own town. He wept outside that house in sympathy for the grief of two sisters; and a few moments later He called their brother back from the tomb. He demonstrated in those few minutes how completely He was both human and divine. He showed His delight to be with the children of men, to share in their sorrows and to be their joy.

In the village of Bethany pilgrims enter
tomb from which Lazarus after being de
several days came forth at Christ's comma
"He was human . . . He was also divine."

These tombs in the valley of Cedron saw
Christ pass by that night . . . and they witnessed Him dragged back up Mount Zion by
armed men to the prison hole which became
the world's first tabernacle, a stone's throw
from where He had just fed his disciples
with bread turned into Himself.

So we find in almost every Gospel passage that the same Christ who walked, talked, prayed, forgave and wrought cures in Palestine is just as meaningful in the Eucharist. Indeed, the Eucharistic life of Christ is at once the fulfilment and the extension of His life in Palestine. He is as close as the nearest tabernacle.

In a sense the world's first stone tabernacle is in Jerusalem on Mt. Zion*, in the ruins of the house of Caiphas, high priest in the year 33 A.D. It is the recently discovered security prison where Christ spent the last hours of the night on which He instituted the Eucharist.

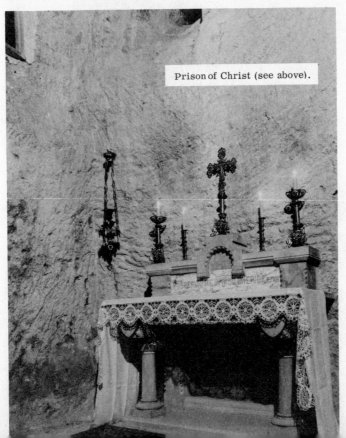

Prison of Christ (see above).

In Bethlehem today, on the very spot where the Infant Christ "lay like a kernel of wheat restored to the straw", a pilgrim receives the Bread of Life. "I felt more fortunate than the wise men or the shepherds," a receiving pilgrim said.

This prison is a box-like structure about twelve feet in diameter and about twelve feet deep. Access was through a hole in the ceiling. The prisoner was lowered into this stone box and the only way to get Him out was with a rope. While the fact of the prison's existence was long known, the actual prison itself was not discovered until a few years ago, together with the scales to weigh the "sin-offerings" and other items which identified the prison area as that of the high priest. A staircase has now been cut into the prison so that the Eucharistic Liturgy can be celebrated in this subterranean hold where on the very night after the institution of the Blessed Sacrament He, by His Presence, made the place a tabernacle. Hidden here, between the hours of the first Mass and its culmination on Calvary, He prayed for us.

To receive the Eucharist in such a holy place could be a special experience. Nonetheless there is hardly a Christian who would not agree with the pilgrim who said: "I spent so much to come to the Holy Land, which seems scarcely to have changed since Christ's day, and it was here I learned what I should have known before I started. He left here places and memories. Himself He left in the Eucharist."

And what about His miracles? Does He still perform them in London and New York, in Berlin and Des Moines, in Bangkok and Athens, as He did in Bethany?

CHAPTER IX

"PROOFS"

OF THE thousands of frescoes, drawings, and inscriptions found in the catacombs from the first centuries of Christianity, *most* refer to miracles* related to the Eucharist. The miracle most frequently depicted is that of the multiplication of loaves and fishes. Pictures of this miracle are even more frequent than the "Breaking of the Bread" (see pages 61-63-64), which is the second most recurring image. Next the catacombs reveal other miracles of Jesus in the following order of frequency: the cure of the Paralytic who was let down through the roof of a house; the resurrection of Lazarus; the cure of a woman with an issue of blood; the cure of a blind man. The fourth most frequently found subject is the adoration of the Magi at Christ's birth, again a miraculous occurrence.

As we mentioned before, miracles were a basis for Christian faith in the "incredible secret." Our Lord Himself had often told them: if they could not believe, they had only to remember the miracles He performed. Hence we can particularly understand the frequency of the pictures of the resurrection of

106

Lazarus because, just before summoning the four-day corpse to life, Christ cried out before the tomb: "Because of the people who stand here . . . *that they may believe* . . ." (John 11,43)

And there is the touching incident, also related by Saint John, of the boy who was born blind. When the Pharisees angrily questioned the parents, the latter were afraid to explain what happened but affirmed that the boy had been born blind and that now he saw. When the Pharisees questioned the boy, saying Christ was a sinner and "We do not know where he is from," the boy answered: "Why, herein is a marvel, that you do not know where he is from and yet he opened my eyes . . . Not from the beginning of the world has it been heard that anyone opened the eyes of a man born blind. If this man were not from God, he could do nothing." (John 9, 30)

But who of us is not made a little edgy and uncomfortable by the word "miracle"? We usually prefer to satisfy ourselves with descriptions and analogies.

When it comes to saying flatly *"I believe in the miracle* (beyond human comprehension and possible only to God), we are left with only the supernatural. We may feel like a child walking into the sea and suddenly finding only water beneath his feet.

Sometimes we argue: If He were really there in

that bit of bread stuff which people receive, He could and would give sight to the blind, hearing to the deaf and perform other miracles just as He did in Palestine. Why the one big miracle of His Presence without the others?

To ask that question is not at all preposterous. Moreover the answer is that He *does* perform miracles through the Eucharist. Indeed in the light of modern facilities of communication and objective medical tests, it seems that Christ performs *more miracles today in His Eucharistic life than He did in Palestine.* But the Space Age is conditioned to publicize only miracles of science. Real miracles rarely make headlines.

Even those of us who do not deny the *possibility* of miracles may hesitate to recognize that miracles *are* an integral part of the Gospel fabric. Though we see that we cannot reject miracles unless we also reject Him and the veracity of the Scriptures, we may murmur the trite phrase: "But the age of miracles is past."

Back in the 5th century St. Augustine wrote: "Miracles are still worked in His Name or by means of the Sacrament . . . but *they are not so popularized or made known as to have the same glory as those first ones."*

Now, fifteen hundred years later in the 20th century, those words apply even more aptly. Some miracles He performs today are so striking that if we examine them with an open mind they leave no room for skepticism.

Although this train of thought may make some readers uneasy, there is no help for it. It would be more comfortable to present the Eucharist in a general and vague light, with soft drapings of sentimentality, without the glaring light of reality to reveal the embarrassing anomaly of miracles.

But the fact is that as Christ performed miracles in His Palestinian life, so He performs them in His Eucharist-life. As we mentioned above, it seems certain that if we add up all the evidence for miracles we find that He performs many more miracles in His Eucharist-life now than He did in Palestine.

One reason these miracles today are not so "popularized or made known", as Augustine puts it, is because they are not witnessed in the same way as they were in Palestine. Five thousand men, not counting women and children, were on the mountain by the Sea of Galilee when He created matter from nothing. But today the Eucharistic Christ is approached by single persons, one by one. The meeting between Christ and man now is *personal*. Only in such places as Lourdes and Fatima do we see the Eucharistic Christ today surrounded by vast throngs who cry out "Lord, that I may see!", "Son of David, have mercy on me!" There, of course, is where we are most likely to witness Christ the Miracleworker.

But even miracles at great Eucharistic gather-

ings are scantily publicized. The press gives short
space to Lourdes or Fatima or any other such place,
despite the fact that millions of people visit these
shrines, thousands have been cured there, and non-
partisan medical commissions have judged the miracles.

An invalid coming to Lourdes usually registers
at the *Bureau des Constatations Medicales*. If he
does register upon arrival, and if he subsequently
claims a cure, his before-and-after state is examined
and assessed. The examining doctors are unpaid,
independent men. The President is the only medical man permanently attached to the Bureau. Any
doctor of any nationality, of any belief, or of no belief, is free to enter the Bureau, make whatever in-
quiries he chooses, and be present when any case or
alleged case is being investigated. Pious people who
imagine cures, or hysterical people who are cured
by suggestion, are quickly dismissed. Despite all this,
there are cures which no natural cause whatever is
capable of producing.

Lourdes being a place where the Virgin appeared is of course a center of devotion to her. But
it is consequently, and above all, a center of devotion
to Christ's Presence in the Eucharist. Most cures occur during the procession of the Eucharist.

It would take more than the extent of this book
to report even the most outstanding Eucharistic miracles, so rather than enumerate many we may at least

give details[1] of one witnessed by Dr. Alexis Carrel, the first American to win the Nobel Prize for physiology and medicine. His biography fills the better part of a page in Collier's encyclopedia. He was particularly distinguished as an experimental surgeon and biologist and he won the Nordhoff-Jung Cancer Prize in 1931, the Newman Foundation Award in 1937 and the United States Distinguished Service Medal.

In a day when less was known about the human brain and heart than is known today, he kept a heart alive for years outside an animal's body. He pried deep into secrets of man, into the very nature of the brain and the coordination of the sympathetic and parasympathetic nervous systems as the bases of temperament and disease; into nutrition, disease, mental illness, motivation, habit and conditioned reflexes.

Withal he found the time to write a number of books. One of them, *Man the Unknown,* won him international renown not only as a surgeon but as a writer. Published simultaneously in Paris and New York, it soon became a Best Seller. Among his other

[1] Condensation of pp. 24-47 THE VOYAGE TO LOURDES by Anne Carrel.
Copyright 1950 by Anne Carrel
Reprinted by permission of Harper & Row, Publishers, Incorporated.
This version appeared originally in the September 1950 issue of **Reader's Digest.**

books were: *Anastomosis and the Transplantation of Blood Vessels, The Preservation of Tissues, The Transplantation of Limbs, The Transplantation of Veins and Organs.*

At one time, for what he called "purely scientific reasons", Dr. Carrel decided to go to Lourdes, and he quoted himself as saying just before his departure for the shrine: "If God exists, miracles are possible. But does God exist objectively? How am I to know? *To the scientific mind a miracle is an absurdity.*"

When somebody asked him what kind of miracle he would have to see to be sure that God existed, Carrel answered: "An organic disease cured . . . a cancer disappearing, a congenital dislocation suddenly vanishing."

On his journey to Lourdes he proposed to be "entirely objective", and he did not think it likely that he would admit a miracle even if the many sick people on the train in which he traveled were suddenly cured, because most of them probably were suffering from nervous and traumatic hysterias.

However, one patient obviously was dying from organic disease. Her name was Marie Ferrand. "If such a case as hers were cured," wrote Dr. Carrel, "it would indeed be a miracle. I would never doubt again."

With permission of THE READER'S DIGEST and of HARPERS, publishers of Dr. Carrel's account of his trip entitled JOURNEY TO LOURDES, here is what the surgeon wrote after he went to the infirmary at Lourdes to examine Marie Ferrand. In the account he refers to himself by name, spelling Carrel backward.

"Her head, with its white emaciated face, was flung on the pillow. Her wasted arms lay flat at her sides. Her breathing was rapid and shallow.

" 'How are you feeling?' Lerrac asked her gently.

"She turned her dim, dark-circled eyes toward him and her gray lips moved in an inaudible reply.

"Taking her hand, Lerrac put his fingertips on her wrist. Her pulse was excessively rapid and irregular. Her heart was giving out. 'Get me the hypodermic syringe,' he told the nurse. 'We'll give her an injection of caffeine.'

"Pulling back the covers the nurse removed the cradle that held up the bedclothes and the rubber ice bag which hung over the patient's abdomen. Marie Ferrand's emaciated body lay exposed again, her abdomen distended as before. The solid masses were still there; at the center, under the umbilicus, he could still feel the fluid. As the caffeine entered her thin thigh, Marie Ferrand's face contracted suddenly.

"Lerrac turned to A.B. 'It's just what I told you,' he added, "advanced tuberculous peritonitis. She may last a few days more, but she is doomed. Death is very near.'

"As Lerrac turned to leave, the nurse stopped

During the Ecumenical Council many Bishops joined the throngs before the Eucharistic presence in the grotto of Lourdes. Although identical to the same presence in churches all over the world, here there is accurate record kept of miraculous cures like that seen by Dr. Carrell.

him. 'Doctor, is it all right to take Marie Ferrand to the pool?'

"Lerrac looked at her in amazement. 'What if she dies on the way?' he said.

" 'She is absolutely determined to be bathed. She came all the way for this.'

"At that moment Dr. J., who practiced in a town outside Bordeaux and had accompanied his own patients to Lourdes, entered the ward. Lerrac asked his opinion about having Marie Ferrand carried to the pool. Once again the covers were removed and Dr. J. examined Marie Ferrand. "She's at the point of death,' he said finally in a low voice. "She might very well die at the Grotto.'

" 'You see, mademoiselle,' said Lerrac, 'how imprudent it would be to take this patient to the pool. However, I have no authority here; I cannot give permission, or refuse it.'

" 'The girl has nothing to lose,' said the Mother Superior. 'It would be cruel to deprive her of the supreme happiness of being taken to the Grotto, though I fear she may not live to reach it. We shall take her there now, in a few minutes.'

" 'I will be at the pool myself in any case,' said Lerrac. 'If she goes into a coma, send for me.'

" 'She will certainly die,' Dr. J. repeated as they left the ward.''

Dr. Carrel's account then goes on to describe the pools of Lourdes, and he says that he was standing outside the pools when Marie Ferrand was brought to be lowered into the waters. His narrative continues:

"For a moment, before going to the pool, they lowered the stretcher to the ground. The sick girl was apparently unconscious. Lerrac put his hand on her wrist. Her pulse was more rapid than ever, her face ashen. It was obvious that this young girl was about to die. He wondered how it would affect the pilgrims if she died in the pool. What would they think of miracles then?"

Marie Ferrand was not cured. But neither had she died. Nothing had happened. Many dramatic cures at Lourdes follow exactly the same pattern.

Dr. Carrel remarks this fact and then describes the ceremonies which followed, leading up to the great moment when all the sick are assembled at the Grotto to receive *the blessing of Christ in the Eucharist*.

He tells how he "walked past the little carts and through the crowd toward the Grotto. Pausing for a moment at the edge of the stream he observed the crowd. A young intern from Bordeaux, Mr. M., whom Lerrac had met the day before, greeted him. 'Have you any cures?' Lerrac asked.

" 'No,' replied M. 'A few of the hysteria cases have recovered, but there has been nothing unexpected, nothing that one can't see any day in a hospital.'

" 'Come and look at my patient,' said Lerrac. 'Her case is not unusual but I think she is dying. She is at the Grotto.'

" 'I saw her a few minutes ago,' said M. 'What a pity they let her come to Lourdes.'

"It was now about half-past two. Beneath the rock of Massabielle, the Grotto glittered in the light of its thousand candles. Beyond the high iron grille was a statue of the Virgin, standing in the hollowed rock where Bernadette once saw the glowing vision of the lady in white, the Immaculate Conception. In front of the iron grille and almost touching it, Lerrac recognized the slender figure of Marie Ferrand's nurse. He and M. made their way through the crowd and, stopping near Marie Ferrand's stretcher, leaned against the low wall. She was motionless, her breathing still rapid and shallow; she seemed to be at the point of death. More pilgrims were approaching the Grotto. Volunteers and stretcher-bearers came crowding in. The little carts were being wheeled from the pools to the Grotto.

"Lerrac glanced again at Marie Ferrand. Suddenly he stared. It seemed to him that there had been a change, that the harsh shadows on her face had disappeared, that her skin was somehow less ashen. Surely, he thought, this was hallucination. But the hallucination itself was interesting psychologically;

hastily he jotted down the time in his notebook. It was twenty minutes before three. But if the change in Marie Ferrand was an hallucination, it was the first one Lerrac had ever had. He turned to M. 'Look at our patient again,' he said. 'Does it seem to you that she has rallied a little?'

" 'She looks much the same to me,' answered M. 'All I can see is that she is no worse.'

"Leaning over the stretcher, Lerrac took her pulse again and listened to her breathing. 'The respiration is less rapid,' he told M. after a moment.

" 'That may mean that she is about to die,' said M.

"Lerrac made no reply. To him it was obvious that there was a sudden improvement in her general condition. Something was taking place. He stiffened to resist a tremor of emotion, and concentrated all his powers of observation on Marie Ferrand. He did not lift his eyes from her face. A priest was preaching to the assembled throngs of pilgrims and patients; hymns and prayers burst out sporadically (the Blessed Sacrament was reserved in the Grotto), and in this atmosphere of fervor, under Lerrac's cool, objective gaze, the face of Marie Ferrand slowly continued to change. Her eyes, so dim before, were now wide with ecstacy as she turned them toward the Grotto. The change was undeniable. The nurse leaned over and held her.

"Suddenly, Lerrac felt himself turning pale. The blanket which covered Marie Ferrand's distended abdomen was gradually flattening out. 'Look at her abdomen!' he exclaimed to M.

"M. looked. 'Why yes,' he said, 'it seems to have gone down. It's probably the folds in the blanket that give that impression.'

"The bell of the basilica had just struck three. A few minutes later, there was no longer any sign of distention in the girl's abdomen.

"Lerrac felt as though he were going mad.

"Standing beside Marie Ferrand, he watched the intake of her breath and pulsing of her throat with fascination. The heartbeat, though still very rapid, had become regular.

" 'How do you feel?' he asked her.

" 'I feel very well,' she answered in a low voice. 'I am still weak, but I feel I am cured.'

"There was no longer any doubt: Marie Ferrand's condition was improving so much that she was scarcely recognizable . . .

"The crowd at the Grotto was not even aware that it had happened.

"It was the resurrection of the dead; it was a miracle!

"Lerrac went back to his hotel, forbidding himself to draw any conclusions until he could find out exactly what had happened . . .

"At half past seven he started for the hospital,

tense and on fire with curiosity. One question alone filled his mind: Had the incurable Marie Ferrand been cured?

"Opening the door of the ward of the Immaculate Conception (Hospital) he hastened across the room to her bedside. With mute astonishment, he stood and gazed. The change was overpowering. Marie Ferrand, in a white jacket, was sitting up in bed. Though her face was still gray and emaciated, it was alight with life; her eyes shone; a faint color tinted her cheeks. Such an indescribable serenity emanated from her person that it seemed to illuminate the whole sad ward with joy. 'Doctor,' she said, 'I am completely cured. I feel very weak, but I think I could even walk.'

"Lerrac put his hand on her wrist. The pulse beat was calm and regular. Her respiration had also become completely normal. Confusion flooded Lerrac's mind. Was this merely an apparent cure, the result of a patient's stimulus of auto-suggestion? Or was it a new fact, an astounding unacceptable event —a miracle? For a brief moment, before subjecting Marie Ferrand to the supreme test of examining her abdomen, Lerrac hesitated. Then, torn between hope and fear, he threw back the blanket. The skin was smooth and white. Above the narrow hips was the small, flat, slightly concave abdomen of a young, undernourished girl. Lightly he put his hands on the wall of the abdomen, looking for traces of the distention and the hard masses he had found before. They had vanished like a bad dream.

"The sweat broke out on Lerrac's forehead. He felt as though someone had struck him on the head. His heart began to pump furiously. He held himself in with iron determination.

"He had not heard Doctor J. and M. entering the ward. Suddenly he noticed them, standing beside him. 'She seems to be cured,' he said, then, 'I cannot find anything wrong. Please examine her yourselves.'

"While his two colleagues carefully palpated Marie Ferrand's abdomen, Lerrac stood aside and watched them with shining eyes. There could be no doubt whatever that the girl was cured. It was a miracle, the kind of miracle which took the public by storm and sent them in hordes to Lourdes. And the public was justified in its enthusiasm. Whatever the source of these cures, the results were not only breathtaking but positive and good. Again it swept over Lerrac how fortunate he was, that among all the patients at Lourdes that day it was the one he had known and studied carefully whom we saw cured!"

There follows a description of the scientistdoctor's personal reaction. What would his fellowscientists think of a man who believed in miracles? Would any one of them believe who had not seen it for themselves? Dr. Carrel concludes: "When a scientist tried to apply his intellectual techniques and convictions to metaphysics, he was lost. He could no longer use his reasoning, since reason did not go beyond the establishing of facts and their relations to each other. In the search for causes, there was nothing absolute, there were no signposts along the way, there was no proof of right or wrong. All things in this mysterious realm were therefore possible. Intellectual systems no longer seemed to count. In the face of life and death, the mere theories were void. It was not science that nourished the inner life of man; it was the faith of the soul. He had to reach a conclusion. He was certain of his diagnosis. It was incontestable that a miracle had taken place. But was it by the hand of God? Some day he would know. Meanwhile, it was safe to say it was a cure; that much he could guarantee. Yet deep within himself, he felt that was not all . . .

"He climbed the steps of the church in the glitter of lights while the organ boomed and a thousand voices chanted. He sat down on a chair at the back near an old peasant. For a long time he sat there motionless, his hands over his face, listening to the hymns. Then he found himself praying: '. . . I believe in Thee. Thou didst answer my prayers by a blazing miracle. I am still blind to it. I still doubt. But the greatest desire of my life is to believe, to believe passionately, implicitly, and never more to analyze and doubt . . . Beneath the deep, harsh warnings of my intellectual pride a smothered dream persists. Alas, it is still only a dream but the most enchanting of them all. It is the dream of believing in Thee and of loving Thee with the shining spirit of men of God.' "

The notes which Dr. Carrel made are still on record at the Medical Commission in Lourdes.

If the great scientist, Carrel, had not been at Lourdes that day, who would ever have heard of Marie Ferrand and her cure? One of the most significant facts in the entire account is in the two sentences: "The crowd at the Grotto *was not even aware* that it happened. It was the resurrection of the dead; it was a miracle!"

Many of the miracles Christ performs now in His Eucharistic state are even more dramatic than that of Marie Ferrand. There was a worker from Belgium with a piece of bone missing in his leg, his ankle and foot dangled, suspended only by flesh and tendons, so that it could be turned a hundred and eighty degrees. That missing bone was *instantly created in his leg*. The doctors had before-and-after x rays. When the man died, an autopsy showed where the new bone had come to unite with the separated bone. The full documentation and x-rays can be seen at the office of the Medical Commission at Lourdes, together with the affirmation of many witnesses.

When this American Bishop blessed the sick at Fatima, May 13, 1950, a paralytic was cured.

Dr. Carrel was so deeply moved because he was a *witness*. The writer can add the account of two apparent miracles which he himself witnessed, which partially explains his desire to write this book.

The patient in the first case was a man in Lisbon, Portugal, who suffered from Parkinson's disease. As the creeping paralysis rose from his lower limbs, advancing closer and closer to the heart, the patient was plunged into deep melancholy. His wife pleaded with him repeatedly to go only ninety miles away to Fatima. In mockery, because he knew that, like himself, his attending physician did not believe in miracles, he said to his wife in the doctor's presence: "I'll go if he does."

It occurred to the doctor that a trip to the church at Fatima* might cheer his patient, or at least it would be a temporary distraction, so he surprised the ill man by saying: "All right, let's go."

The six apparitions of the Virgin Mary at Fatima took place on the 13th day of six consecutive months, so that day is particularly celebrated at the Shrine. As this was the 13th day of October there was a large crowd of pilgrims. The non-believing doctor and his non-believing patient were among the first in the rows of invalids. I (the writer of this book) was carrying the canopy over the Holy Eucharist as It was raised by the priest to bless the patient.

The man suddenly pushed himself up in his wheelchair. Trembling, he began to move and feel his legs. Then he cried out to those around him: *"I am not dreaming, am I? I am not dreaming?"*

This writer's reaction was something like the reaction of thousands of television viewers in the first moment they saw the murder of Lee Harvey Oswald, during a live news program following the assassination of President Kennedy in 1963. *It did not seem real.*

The doctor's mouth fell open in amazement as he slowly sank to his knees. Tears began to roll down his cheeks. "This was not for you," he exclaimed through sobs. "This was for me."

Some years later I witnessed another apparent miracle in the same place. The patient this time was a woman twenty-two years old named Arminda dos Campos. She had been ill for nine years and had undergone seven major operations. She had a greatly distended abdomen, total paralysis and an opening in her side cut by a surgeon's scalpel to drain purulent matter. Again I was standing very close to the patient. In fact, I was standing directly in front of her at the moment of her cure and saw the blankets flatten on her body, saw her sit up, and within two hours *I saw the scars which had instantaneously formed in the place of the incisions.*

In another book [1] I recorded my own reactions to seeing the scars within an hour of the cure: As

---

[1] "Russia Will Be Converted" (See last page).

This girl was instantaneously cured of a tumor in the brain. The cure was witnessed by the author of this book and is described in detail in "Russia Will Be Converted." Edge of the monstrance containing the Eucharist is seen at edge of face in foreground.

I stood near the side of the table opposite the Bishop, the cured girl was introduced from the end of the table by one of the nurses. The Bishop of Fatima listened patiently. In his twenty-six years as Bishop he had heard many similar stories. He had gone into sheaves of endless details about cures.

Then I heard the nurse saying: "Show the Bishop the scars where the fistulas were.'

There, on the upper part of the thigh, at a spot revealed with careful modesty, were two clear, dry scars. They were not red as a freshly healed wound usually is. They were clear (like a little scar on my own hand . . . more than thirty years old). One of them was so deep that it would have been possible to insert the tip of one's little finger where the opening had been.

After staring at the healed tissue, wondering if it could have been possible that there were really awful sores there just a few hours before, I saw the face of the nurse. Tears were streaming down her cheeks. With an open-arm gesture and trembling hands, suddenly she exclaimed: "And Your Excellency, to think that this morning I put bandages there on large running openings!"

It was only in that final moment . . . looking into the tear-stained face of the nurse . . . that the miracle made its full impact. In that moment I believed with all my heart that we in that room were experiencing the same wonder experienced

"Son of David, have mercy on me!"

when Christ healed the nine lepers, or when the blind man shouted out that suddenly he could see. We were, I felt absolutely sure, seeing it with our own eyes—not two thousand years ago, but *now*. We were objectively experiencing the reality of the Eucharist, *the reality of Christ among us.*

To understand this reality we keep returning to the miracle of the Last Supper.

Basilica of St. John, Lateran, site of first public central building of the Church given to Pope Sylverius by Constantine in 315 A.D. Part of table of Last Supper is said to be under altar and Pope celebrates Eucharistic liturgy here on anniversary of the Last Supper: Maundy Thursday.

CHAPTER X

WHY WE HAVE THE SECRET NOW

WATERPOTS ARE often seen in Catacomb pictures. They may indicate the miracle of Cana or they may be meant to recall the great act of humility and love with which Christ began the last supper.

Just before that meal was to begin, Christ laid aside His outer garments. He girded Himself with a towel. Then He poured water in a basin and went from one apostle to another, washing each man's feet and drying them with the towel which hung from His waist.

On Maundy* Thursday of 1964, while this book was being written, Pope Paul VI performed the age-old ceremony as it is performed every year. He removed his outer vestments, descended the Papal throne in the apse of St. John Lateran* to wash the feet of certain people present. They happened to be five Mexicans, one Cuban, one Chilean, one Paraguayan and others from Latin American countries, a total of thirteen. [1]

---

[1] This number thirteen is not a mistake. The number was orig-

Many find this washing a moving sight. It strikes them as dramatic that the Pope, the supreme pontiff of Christendom, should kneel to perform such a menial task for them. And yet, how faint a picture this is of what Christ did.

The feet of modern men are usually clean. In fact, since the men to be washed by the Pope are selected in advance, they carefully scrub their feet to prepare for the ritual. The washing is not physically necessary.

But the feet of the men at the Last Supper were dirty. How could they be otherwise? The apostles had been walking all day along the dusty roads leading to Jerusalem and also over the spittle and dung strewn city streets. In short, it was a nasty job that Christ undertook, a job quite different from the ceremonial ablution which the Pope annually performs in Christendom's first church.

Why did Christ do it?

Peter protested the act. He thought it unseemly, even shocking that Christ, the Son of God, should minister to them in such a lowly manner.

Admittedly the job had to be done. In those days when people reclined at table, the couches

---

inally twelve, but on one occasion in the early days of the Lateran church when the Pope began to wash the feet of the deacons who had been chosen, he counted thirteen men instead of twelve. To the amazement of all it was an apparition of Christ, Who after the washing disappeared. So now thirteen are selected in the Lateran church to commemorate the event.

would have become soiled from dusty feet. But usually people washed their own feet unless they were affluent enough to pay a servant to do it for them.

Christ gave His reason. He washed the feet of the apostles to show them that they must love one another and be humble in their attitude toward one another. He spelled it out in exact words: "If then I, being your Lord and Master, washed your feet, you also ought to wash one another's feet. For I have given you an example that as I have done to you, so you do also."

A few minutes later He expatiated: "A new commandment I give unto you: that you love one another as I have loved you . . . By this shall all men know that you are My disciples, if you have love one for another."

Christ had a second reason also: He did it because He Himself loved them so much that He yearned to express His feeling in any way that presented itself. After all, service is love made manifest. Christ became the servant to show that nothing was too insignificant, nothing too great for Him to do for them.

Love filled Him. "Having loved His own, He loved them to the end." He loved until His last few hours on earth, until His very death on the cross. Then this love burst forth into soaring words which have haunted the world like an unforgettable melody ever since: *"As the Father loves Me, so I love you.*

Abide in My love."

Yes, love was the theme song of His every act and word that night: love of the Father for Him, His love for the Father in the Holy Spirit, His love for man and men's love for one another.

All this was the prelude to the great Act of Love, the giving of Himself under the appearance of their ordinary foodstuffs.

"JESUS TOOK BREAD, BLESSED AND BROKE AND GAVE IT TO HIS DISCIPLES SAYING: *'Take and eat, this is My body'*, and taking a cup He gave thanks and gave it to them saying: *'All of you drink of this, for this is My blood of the new covenant which is being shed for many unto the forgiveness of sins.'* " (Matt. 26,26-28)

Early Christians were able to accept this because they saw love as the key to God's relationship with man. The apostle John had written that God *is* love. They saw that love, especially divine love, tends to share and to give, and that every action of God, indeed His very Being in Trinity, is an expression of love and of giving. One wants to consume the beloved.

Modern man, for reasons too profound and too ramified to explore here, often has become alienated from God. There seems to be a general feeling that God is not interested in the affairs of man, and in this atmosphere the acceptance of a divine love which would go to the point of a sharing such as Christ declared is simply out of grasp. For this reason many Christians, although believing in Christ and accepting the Bible as an honest and believable account of all that Christ did and said, take refuge in the idea that He did not mean His words literally. They think that He meant to say this represents My body, rather than what He did say: "this is" My body.

As mentioned in the last chapter, we must have the assumption that the reader either believes and wants to understand more of the world's greatest secret, or that he does not believe, *but for the sake of understanding is willing at this point to take a position of belief.*

Since the Eucharist, and all other mysteries of Faith, fit like the spokes of a wheel into the central mystery of the Triune God's loving nature, the Eucharist cannot be grasped even remotely without some understanding of God Himself. Most Christians who find difficulty in believing Christ's words about Himself as food probably do not disbelieve God's ability to perform such a miracle, but cannot believe *that He loves man that much.*

During that historic Last Supper, Christ told His disciples about this. He revealed to them the nature of God*. He told them that God is love, and that love is the explanation of His being with them. He even demonstrated it. He washed their feet, like a servant, before telling them unequivocally that "I and the Father are One . . . when you see Me, you see the Father also."

Every word Christ spoke at that first Eucharistic Liturgy was a word of love. The disciples felt it, even though they could not understand. Today, many of us understand but do not feel.

Theologians today use the word "circumincession" to express the complete and reciprocal interchange of life and love which flows between the three Persons without beginning and without end . . . an interchange reflected in the Eucharist which Christ revealed to us that night.

Each of the three Persons, possessing the loving nature, took a distinct part in the institution of the Blessed Sacrament. The Father gave the Son: "The Father sent Me," Christ said. The Son gave the Eucharist: "This is My body." And the Holy Spirit reached out to men and made possible their mental and spiritual acceptance of such a mystery: "It is expedient that I go . . . I will send the Paraclete, and He will make It known to you."

So the reason for the Eucharist is found in the nature of God: *God's love*. This alone ultimately makes the world's greatest secret understandable. *The loving nature of God desired to give us His very Self*.

Love can be given in half measures from man to man, but God gives all: Himself.

He unites with us; He unites us to Him. Love always tends to union. Through the Eucharist we are joined to God, and through Him to our fellow Christians. "That you may be one even as the Father and I are one," was the way that Christ expressed it.

Father Walter Burghardt[1] describes a day during World War II when "A tremendous event took place over the face of the earth. That day Christ, our Lord, hiding His Godhead and His manhood under the appearance of bread, pillowed His head on the tongue of a child in Baltimore's Cathedral. The same day the same Christ slipped past bursting shells and past the lips of a Marine in the Marshalls. The same day Christ braved the beaches of Normandy to rest His brow beneath a British helmet. The same Christ made His home next to the throbbing heart of an Italian peasant woman and bent low to a bomb shelter in Berlin. The same Christ rode with a pilot in the cockpit of a Japanese Zero fighter and fed the brave on a Burma road. Even the barbed wire could not keep the same Christ from lighting up a brown face in Bataan."

Christ came that day also to the Pope, to presidents of nations, labor unions, corporations. He made all these people one in the love which is Himself, the Giver of the Eucharist, the Sacrament of Love.

Yes, only love . . . *an infinite love* . . . can explain it.

[1] ALL LOST IN WONDER, Newman Press, 1961, p.93.

CHAPTER XI

THE SACRIFICE

EARLY CHRISTIANS even found a way to symbolize the identity of the Eucharistic Liturgy with sacrifice: An altar with three legs as traditionally used for the bloody sacrifices of old.

Today there may seem little resemblance between the Eucharistic Liturgy and the liturgy that the gospels describe as the last supper. Nonetheless, it is only the "trimmings" which have changed. In the essential part, there has been no substantial change whatever.

From the beginning Christians let their enthusiasms and their inspiration of the moment guide them in the peripheral parts, that is in the parts of the liturgy before and after the "Secret." The secret part, celebrated in a similar manner wherever Christians gathered for worship, was a repetition of what Christ Himself had given the apostles that last night. It is the same today, and it was the same in the first years of Christianity. We see this fact confirmed again and again by the many symbols and pictures which have come to light in the recently unearthed catacombs.

139

In the Catacombs of Sts. Peter and Marcellinus is this very early "breaking of bread". Notice the altar with three legs in front of the banquet table . . . the same kind of altar used for bloody sacrifice before the Eucharistic liturgy.

On that night of nights before Christ died He asked them to do as He was doing then "in commemoration" of Him. So His followers made the Eucharistic Liturgy a fulfillment of that, His final request. Acting for the great High Priest, Christ, the priest, pronounces in His name the identical words that Christ used: *"This is My body"* . . . *"This is My blood"*.

The Eucharistic Liturgy, as a renewal of the Last Supper, must be the most sublime form of worship to be found in today's world because the participants do not worship alone; they worship "by Him, and with Him, and in Him." Prayers of one's own invention said from now until that day when Gabriel's horn shall sound in the heavens, even if numbered in astronomical figures, could not be as sublime as one celebration of the Eucharistic Liturgy. Obviously The Mass* is Christ's prayer; it is His sacrifice; it is His worship. It is of an order different from any purely human act; it is Divine, and the Christian's faith assures him that he actually participates in it!

Throughout history the Eucharistic Liturgy (or the Mass) has been understood to be a universal form of worship, even though it is said in local languages. It has always included "all Christians, living and dead", particularly "all true believers" as well as "us sinners". It has been and is like a huge sym-

In Orvieto, Italy, Pope Paul VI lifts the Eucharistic chalice before a piece of cloth on which drops of blood streamed from a Host broken by a doubting priest. The words the Pope has just spoken over the chalice are identical to those words of Christ at the last supper and by all priests who celebrate the same liturgy: "This is My Blood".

phony orchestra in which all join to make harmonious melody for and to and through God.

To some people since the Reformation the official character of the Eucharistic Liturgy may seem to have become too stylized. So Vatican Council II gave great attention to a tendency to use private prayers even during the Mass. Too many had lost sight of the fact that the *official* character of the Eucharistic Liturgy lends weight to the prayer and to the worship.

Perhaps an analogy may help clarify this.

If a man's barber were to present him with a medal in the name of the United States Congress, might not the presentation be taken as a joke? But if this barber were authorized by Congress to present the medal, even in the Capitol building, it would be a great official honor.

The official Eucharistic Liturgy is solemn to Christians because Christ authorized it. So is it not fitting that the most solemn breaking of the bread be set in a fairly elaborate framework of prayers, hymns, sermons, scriptural readings and so on, not unlike the setting given by Christ Himself the night before He died?

To some readers who know the Eucharistic liturgy the following description of it will seem unnecessary. But to others it may seem the most significant part of this book because it describes the Last Supper rite as the central religious act of millions of persons around the world today.

Presented with a questionnaire to evaluate this book before publication, one non-Christian said of this section:

"Being a non-Christian I found myself becoming quite engrossed; it made me understand this rite which is actually very secret outside of the Church."

As we might expect, the explanation begins in the New Testament.

In the second chapter of the *Acts of The Apostles*,[1] St. Luke speaks of the brethren "persevering in the doctrine of the apostles and in the communication of the breaking of bread, and in prayers." In the first epistle to Timothy[2] as well as in the first epistle to the Thessalonians[3], St. Paul exhorts the brethren to read his epistles and "to attend to reading and to doctrine" in connection with the Eucharistic feast. Also we see in the ACTS OF THE APOSTLES[4] and in St. Paul's epistles to the Corinthians[5] and to the Ephesians[6] that when Christians gathered together for worship and to celebrate the Eucharistic feast, there were psalms, hymns and sermons. The famous passage from St. Paul's first letter to the Corinthians[7] actually gives an outline of the breaking of the bread in thanksgiving that followed the earlier part of the service. Then in his letter to the Hebrews[8] he

[1]Acts 2:42   [4]Acts 20:7   [5]I Cor. 14:26   [7]I Cor. 11:20-9
[2]Tim. 4:13   [3]Thess. 5:27   [6]Eph. 5:19   [8]Heb. 13:10

...igrims participate in a Mass celebrated in the catacombs where Peter and Paul said Mass, where one is surrounded by tombs for first martyrs, where the first symbols of the Eucharist are frescoed into the walls. Not much has changed except the costumes of the community.

speaks of the table of the Eucharist being an altar.

So Dr. Fortescue, Ph.D., S.T.D., the great liturgical scholar of England, could write (C.E.Vol. 9 p.307): "We have already in the New Testament all the essential elements that we find later in the organized liturgies; lessons on the psalms, hymns, sermons, prayers, consecration, communion."

As we said above, the Eucharistic liturgy was more fluid than it is today. Some scriptural readings were probably a matter of choice of the individual priest. Those with a Jewish background might naturally have stressed what was read in the synagogues, and among the Gentiles the letters of Peter, Paul and James were certainly read over and over.

Today parts of all these readings have been standardized into the present liturgy.

Fortunately the apostle John has left us a detailed, eyewitness account of what Christ did at the Last Supper, as we described in Chapter IV.

That Passover Supper was an offering by Christ to the Father, through the Holy Spirit, of His Body and Blood. Also it was the giving of His Body and Blood to men and for men for the remission of sins, for salvation.

A moment's thought shows that the same definition also fits the offering of Calvary.

That, too, was a love offering by Christ to the Father, through the Holy Spirit, of His Body and

Blood and an offering made for men for the remission of sins.

Thus Christian theologians from the very early days of the Church, from the very time of the apostles themselves, saw that on Calvary Christ was the High Priest Who made the offering or sacrifice, and that in the Eucharistic Liturgy He again becomes the High Priest Who makes the offering or sacrifice. On Calvary, the "victim", or the offering was Christ Himself, His body and blood; in the Eucharistic Liturgy, the "Victim" or the thing offered is also Christ Himself, His Body and Blood. The very word "host" means sacrifice.

A single point of difference made by Christians between Calvary and the Eucharistic Liturgy is the manner in which the offering is made. On Calvary Christ's body and blood were visibly offered. There was a death which bystanders could witness, an offering reminiscent of the Old Testament immolations; the lamb was slaughtered and destroyed. In the Eucharistic Liturgy Christians knew that Christ did not die again, but offered Himself, the Lamb of God, and thus immolated or sacrificed His Body and Blood in a mystical (hidden) manner under the appearances of bread and wine.

On Calvary Christ died for men's sins. He offered Himself in atonement that men might then, through His atonement or redemption, have a chance to try for heaven, a chance which primeval sin

had lost for the human race. In the Eucharistic
Liturgy His death applies to men's souls the graces
that He has won for them in proportion to their spiritual capacity.

By receiving the Eucharist Christians believed
they were intimately united with Christ and offered
themselves with Him to the Father through the Holy
Spirit. In Peter's words[1] we are "a royal priesthood",
for we are then co-offerers. Through the robed priest
at the altar who speaks for us, and through our High
Priest the Lord and Saviour Jesus Christ, we make
the offering He makes to God the Father. Through
Him Whom we receive into our hearts and souls in
the Eucharist, we offer ourselves. If we give ourselves to Him as completely as He gives Himself to
us, sincerely desiring to retain nothing of ourselves,
He will lavish His grace upon us so abundantly as to
make us into His image, into saints, "for this is the
Will of God, your sanctification."

Some argue as to which is more important in
the Eucharistic Liturgy, sacrifice or communion.*
St. Thomas Aquinas argued for the latter.[2] Vatican
Council II reasserted the importance of participation in the entire Eucharistic Liturgy, but communion is the high point.

"Except you eat my flesh and drink my blood,"

---

[1] I Epistle St. Peter II,9.   [2] Summa III, q.79,a.1,

Christ said, "you shall not have life in you." (John 6:54)

Saint Thomas says that *no one* possesses grace before he receives this sacrament at least in desire, "his own in the case of an adult, that of the Church in the case of infants."[1]

Thus St. Thomas, who was singled out by Pope John XXIII before Vatican Council II as the chief authority to be considered in this matter, stresses that *all* other sacraments are dependent upon this one. To receive Christ in this sacrament we are baptized and confirmed. To make it possible, priests are ordained. Even marriage, as an element in the visible structure of the Church, serves to represent communion in human terms.

After Vatican Council II turned the altars around and drew the communities into active participation in the sacrifice, communions increased. But in 1966 *less than half* of those who attended Mass *went to Communion.* Millions missed Mass altogether (over five million in Italy alone). For this reason there appears urgent need for increase of private devotions and especially of sacramentals. Such is the burden of the message of Fatima.

Saint Thomas says that sacramentals (such as the Rosary and the Scapular) play an *essential role*

[1] Summa III, q.79,a.1,ad1

in the liturgy by helping to establish ideal conditions for the reception of the sacraments.[1]

It is worth recalling here the declaration written at the Council of Trent as a summation of what Christians had always believed about the Eucharistic Liturgy from the time of Christ up to the mid-sixteenth century when it was written. It describes exactly what is believed today by a majority of Christians without any change whatever. The declaration, which we quoted earlier, goes like this: "Jesus Christ, our God and Saviour, although He was to offer Himself once and for all to God the Father on the altar of the cross by His death, there to work out our eternal redemption, yet since His priesthood was not to be extinguished by His death, He at the Last Supper, on the night that He was betrayed, wanted to leave to . . . the Church a visible sacrifice. The exigencies of our nature demand it. The sacrifice of God once and for all wrought upon the cross, should be reenacted and its memory abide to the end of the world, and its saving power applied (anew to each generation) for the remission of those sins into which we all fall day by day . . . He offered His Body and Blood to God the Father under the appearance of bread and wine, and gave them under the same appearance to His apostles. These men He then appointed priests of the New Testament—they

[1] Ibidem. Also see **Meeting Christ in the Sacraments,** by Colman E. O'Neill, O.P., Alba House, 1964, pp. 334-335.

and their successors—by His words, 'Do this in remembrance of Me'. So He gave the command to
offer the sacrifice as the Church has understood and
taught."

Now in comparison, here is how the latest Ecumenical Council* affirmed it in 1964:

"At the Last Supper, on the night He was handed over, Our Lord instituted the Eucharistic Sacrifice
of His Body and Blood to perpetuate the sacrifice on
the Cross throughout the ages until He should come,
and thus entrust to the Church, His beloved Spouse,
the memorial of His death and resurrection: A sacrament of devotion, a sign of unity, a bond of charity,
a pascal banquet in which Christ is received, the
soul is filled with Grace and there is given to us
the pledge of future glory" (Constit. "De Sacra Liturgia," C.2.N. Rush A.A.S. LVI, 1964, p. 113).

A modern ecumenical writer puts it well: "At
His death on Calvary, Jesus gave back to His Father
His bodily members nailed to a cross and covered
with blood as a visible expression of His sacrifice
for our sins. Christ gives us His own Body and Blood
in the Holy Eucharist to be offered as a sacrifice commemorating and renewing for all time the Sacrifice
of the Cross. In Holy Communion He draws to Himself all the members of His Mystical Body, the
Church, in order that He may give them as a sacrificial gift to the Father. Thus, by the great power of
His love, He wishes to join us in a living union with

Ecumenical Council Vatican II restored some parts of Eucharistic liturgy to early Christian form, although the heart of the Secret has never changed.

His Mystical Body as one sacrifice, so that Body may grow . . ."[1]

Sometimes externals of religious practice have caused apparent difficulties among Christians to seem more profound than they really are. The 1966 meeting of the World Council of Churches in Geneva saw strong intervention of the Orthodox* to draw all Christian Churches to unity by turning back to the essential beliefs of early times. The Orthodox themselves, with valid Sacraments, may well be the Provident bridge to ultimate ecumenism*, *even though the peripheral elements of their liturgy are quite different from almost all others.*

More and more we are coming to understand that the outer trappings of the liturgy are of little importance. Vestments for the liturgy were at first the everyday dress of the apostolic era. When styles subsequently changed, this original form of dress remained and became the approved garb.

Modern ceremony has evolved. Action performed a certain way for a number of times often became traditional. Other ceremonies used temporarily were later dropped. One such was the "spiritual exercises" in which people moved by the Holy Spirit prophesied and so on. Another was the agape* or feast of altruistic love, before the Liturgy began.

[1] See THE EUCHARIST IN CATHOLIC LIFE, by Lawrence G. Lovasik, S.V.D.

In the beginning this probably derived from a desire to duplicate the Last Supper which Christ ate with the apostles before He gave them the Sacrament.

Communion at one time was usually given under both forms throughout the entire church, that is under both the bread and the wine. However, since theologians agreed that Christ is wholly present, body, blood, soul and divinity under either form, eventually for convenience sake, and also to emphasize that Christ is wholly present under both forms, the custom of giving Communion under bread only was adopted by most of the Western Church. Some Christians still commonly use both forms and almost all Christians today (especially after Ecumenical Council Vatican II) use them on occasion. Christ used both bread and wine to emphasize the identity of the Eucharist with Calvary, as we have already explained. Small particles were broken off.

It was the custom in those far-off days to use a single loaf of bread. Small particles were broken off for each communicant. Today usually separate hosts* are used and only the one which the priest consumes is necessarily broken.

Parenthetically it also might be noted, though this has nothing to do with the Liturgy proper, that in the first centuries because of the danger of attending liturgical service, the initiated or baptized were sometimes allowed to carry the Consecrated Bread home with them. The next day they could communicate themselves without running the risk of going out to the Mass.* The actual "breaking of the bread", or the Mass, would take place only once or twice a week. After the persecutions ceased and the celebration of the Mass became daily, the practice of taking Hosts to private homes was gradually abolished.

All through the centuries some changes or evolution continued. Different languages have been used. In the earliest days of Christianity Greek rather than Latin was the usual language. Until recently there was a fragment of Greek, the *Kyrie Eleison* prayer, in the Roman or Latin Liturgy.

Very ancient usages generally remain in the Mass. During a sung Mass in which the celebrant is assisted by a deacon and a subdeacon, incense is burned just as it was by the ancient Romans in worshipping their gods and as it was by the Hebrews in their synagogues. Also, as mentioned earlier, since the days of the persecutions when the catechumens were excluded from the breaking of the bread and permitted to stay only for initial prayers, the Mass has been divided into two parts. We have the so-called *Missa Catechumenorum* and the *Missa Fidelium* (the Mass of the Catechumens and the Mass of the Faithful): the Liturgy of the Word and the Liturgy of the Eucharist.

Incidentally, since the most solemn and secret part of the Eucharistic Liturgy was heralded by the dismissal of the catechumens, it is easy to see how the word "Mass" evolved. It is derived from the Latin word for dismissal.

But to return to the discussion of changes. Recently many prayers formerly recited in Latin by a majority of Christians are now recited in the vernacular. When the priest actually distributes the Host* or the "Blessed Sacrament" to the people he now says simply "The Body of Christ" and the communicant acknowledges with the simple profession of faith: "Amen". (But let us repeat what we said just a bit earlier that Christians believe they receive not only the Body and Blood of Christ, but the whole living Christ, the Person of the Saviour with His soul and divinity.)

Variations of the Christian Liturgy include not only these already mentioned but the Liturgy of the Eastern Church was for a thousand years markedly different from that of the Western Church. The so-called Roman Rite, though it has become most widespread, is far from unique. As a matter of fact, the Roman Rite more closely resembles the Protestant Episcopal service than it does some Eastern Rites which are actually included in the membership of the Roman Church.

None of these variations of liturgy, as we have reiterated, touches the essential sacrifice.

From the very first days of Christianity there

were cyclical changes repeated in the liturgy each year. In the first centuries it was seen that prayers and scriptural reading should logically reflect the season or the feast being celebrated. So one section of the Eucharistic Liturgy called the *Proper* was made to vary each day while the rest of the Liturgy, the *Ordinary,* was the same for every day of the year. For instance, the Proper of Easter was and is different in spirit and in wording from that of Christmas. Through the year the Liturgy follows Christ's life and that of His Mother and the other saints.

The so-called "Liturgical Year" begins four weeks before Christmas with Advent. The first four weeks are a period of preparation for the coming, or the advent, of the Lord. We are reminded of the final judgment for our sins and the priest wears the somber purple vestments of penance. But always the essential sacrifice is unchanged. Always and in all actions the words are the same: "This is My Body; this is My Blood". When Christ does come at Christmas all explodes in light and joy. This great feast is followed by such major feasts as the circumcision and naming of the Lord on New Year's Day, then by His first manifestation to the non-Hebrew world, Epiphany or the Feast of the Magi.

After a period of rejoicing lasting some weeks, there follows another somber period, Lent, in which we are asked to do penance. This leads to Palm Sunday and Holy Week in which we recall Christ's first breaking of the bread, His suffering and His death, and finally to the triumph of the Resurrection on Easter Sunday.

After Easter Christians celebrate the feast of the Ascension, followed nine days later by the birthday of the Church, the feast of Pentecost or the Feast of the Coming of the Holy Spirit upon the apostles in the form of tongues of fire.

In these variations of the daily Eucharistic Liturgy, or the Mass, Christians relive the life of Christ as He passed it in Palestine. Pope Pius XII called the liturgical year: "Contact with His Mysteries".[1]

Also there are saints' days throughout the year: St. Patrick's Day and St. Valentine's Day may be among the best known, but these are only two out of over two hundred.

Then occasionally there is a Votive Mass, that is a Mass attuned to a special event or said for a special reason. A Nuptial Mass and a Requiem Mass are Votive Masses for blessing on a marriage and for the repose of a soul.

Certain books help in following the liturgical life. Among the best is a set of Gueranger's LI-TURGICAL YEAR. [2] But if a person lacks the time

---

[1] The encyclical **Mediator Dei.** CTSE ed., Para. 176.
[2] St. Therese of Lisieux said that, after experience she would have restricted all her reading to the Bible, biographies, and this one book. Since the time of St. Therese there are now more scholarly works similar to Gueranger, such as the writings of Jungman and Parsch.

to study that book, he can at least use a Missal when he attends Mass. A Missal, which is a miniature of the same book used by the priest, would help anybody to appreciate the liturgy. It contains the Mass prayers for every day of the year, as well as directions about switching from the *Ordinary* to the *Proper* and back again. The two parts are woven together in a sort of pattern.

The modern Eucharistic Liturgy in the Roman Church opens with an *Ordinary* reading, the *Confiteor* which is a confession of unworthiness and a prayer for forgiveness.

The first *Proper* prayer is the *Introit* and that indicates the feast of the day, or at least sets the tone for it. The *Kyrie* is followed by a magnificent hymn of praise, the *Gloria*.

Now come several *Proper* parts, a *Collect* then a Lesson, a reading from one of the *Epistles* and a reading from the *Gospels*.

Usually on Sundays (though not always) a sermon is interjected here. Following it is the solemn declaration of faith, the *Nicene Creed*. This prayer ends the Mass of the Catechumens or Liturgy of the Word. At this point, in the Eastern rite even today the celebrant calls out "Catechumens depart" and "The doors, the doors, attention to the doors!"

The Mass of the Faithful now also called the Liturgy of the Eucharist, opens with a group of Offertory prayers which are "acts" or expressions of love,

oblation and praise. The unconsecrated wine (with
a few drops of water added to symbolize our union
with Christ) is offered to God. Then the priest
washes his hands to show the need for purity before
making sacrifice. At the Last Supper Christ told
Peter: "If I don't wash you, you shall have no part
with Me."

The *Secret*[1] which follows is a *Proper* prayer
said in a normal voice, and it is followed by the prayer of thanksgiving called the Preface which commemorates Christ's giving thanks before His consecration of the bread and wine.

The Preface ends with the *Sanctus,* which re-
peats three times the word "holy" in honor of the
Trinity.

The next section of the Mass, called the *Canon,*
contains the consecration.* This most solemn moment is immediately preceded by prayers (which,
listed, sound more lengthy than they are) for the
Church, the Pope, the bishop of the diocese, for living persons and in particular for all believers and
for those present. There is a remembrance of the
saints in heaven, particularly the apostles and the
first popes and martyrs. Then comes the heart of
the Mass, the Consecration. The priest says the
sacred words of Christ and then lifts the Host and
the Chalice so that all present can see. The acolyte

[1] Now called "Prayer over the gifts."

rings the sanctuary bell. The faithful adore their God.

This august act is followed by a prayer in remembrance of the dead, a plea for ourselves and for all sinners, and then the Canon or the solemn part of the Mass comes to an end with the prayer: "Through Him, and with Him, and in Him is to Thee God the Father Almighty, in union with the Holy Spirit, all honor and glory forever and ever."

The Lord's Prayer follows. Then further prayers of love, of humility and of desire for the coming of Christ, lead up to Communion. The priest receives before he gives Communion to the congregation. After Communion, the Mass comes to a close fairly rapidly with prayers of thanksgiving.

Today there is considerable emphasis on the Liturgy as a certain means of uniting with Christ. The recent Ecumenical Council, Vatican II, was much preoccupied with the subject, and authorized the use of the vernacular so that the people could participate more actively by reciting the prayers in their native tongue.

However, as has been said so often, the essence of the Mass still remains what it has always been: not the prayers that are said, but the offering or the sacrifice, and a person can unite with that without understanding all the prayers. Moreover, although the recommendation is to go to Mass whenever we can, we can unite with the Mass even if we cannot go. After all there are people behind the Iron and Bamboo Curtains who can never get to Mass. There are mothers of small children, and mothers of handicapped or subnormal children who cannot stir from home except on the rare occasions when they can make arrangements for somebody else to watch over their households. There are people on sickbeds in hospitals and asylums.

Is it not commonly admitted that God takes circumstances into consideration, and takes sincere desire for the act? In other words, if you or I truly cannot go to Mass and Communion on a special day or days, we can offer ourselves, our wills, and our hearts, spiritually in union with Christ's offering in the Mass. Also, we can ask that Christ come to us spiritually in Communion. Whenever we honestly cannot go to Him, will He not come to us, if we want Him? Many children in grade-school learn the prayer: "Since I cannot now receive Thee, dear Jesus, in Holy Communion, come spiritually into my soul, and make it Thine own forever and ever."

Even when we go to Communion daily we can say this prayer at odd moments throughout the day. Surely, it can multiply graces in our souls and give us an awareness of our Guest, Who abides with us spiritually from birth to death provided we do not drive Him away.

Who can measure the grace of God? A spiritual Communion, fervently made by a man in a slave-labor camp, or on the battlefields of the Far East, could win more grace or a greater increase of love and awareness of God than another person's Mass and Communion in church.

Some extremists say that since the Eucharistic Liturgy is "official prayer," more sublime than other forms of divine worship, lesser devotions should be eliminated. But this is like saying that only food sustains life, therefore do away with eating and inject food directly into the bloodstream.

The Eucharistic Liturgy, high point of Christian experience, lasts only twenty to thirty minutes. How can anyone in those few moments attain profound union with God without the aid of supplemental devotion? For many it is impossible. This is confirmed not only by experience but also by the messages of Fatima and Lourdes.

One theologian said he could not believe in Fatima, despite the miracles and the approval of the Church, because of the prophecy that entire nations will be annihilated if people do not pray the Rosary. But a colleague explained it this way:

The salvation of the world is Christ, actually present through the Eucharist. He is man's "Food of Life," and is All-sufficient. But so many men have strayed from any contact with Him that they starve to death, hopelessly. It is as though all the food they needed were on a table, but they lie helplessly on the floor too weak to reach it. They need help not only of the intercession of a fellow human being close to God, but also of the first step toward Christ, that humiliating step of acknowledging weakness and therefore crying out for forgiveness and aid. Millions might read this book, for example, and even find it credible. But how many as a result could actually experience fulfillment of the wonderful promise of the Last Supper?

We do not hesitate now to introduce Fatima because the entire event has been scientifically examined [1] and it is perhaps the most important Eucharistic manifestation of our era.

[1] See **Meet the Witnesses,** AMI Press, 1961.

CHAPTER XII

POWER OF THE SECRET

THE MIRACLES of Christ, as we mentioned before, are the subject of most of the first century frescoes brightly adorning the tombs of those who died for Him.

But it is doubtful whether any of these first Christians, except those actually in Palestine with Our Lord, saw anything as dramatic and convincing as what happened in our own century at Fatima.

Paul Claudel described it as "An Explosion of the Supernatural."

Three children claimed to receive a message from Heaven in a country whose capital had been proclaimed by the Soviet as the "atheist capital of the world." They predicted that *a miracle* would take place *at a certain time,* in a *certain place,* "So that everyone may believe."

Such a thing had never before happened in history.

And the first important vision which these children claimed was that of an angel* holding a Host over a chalice. Blood dripped from the Host into the chalice and the children were struck with awe and fear.

Leaving the Host and the chalice suspended in air, the angel   prostrated himself before them and three times said the prayer which begins: "O most Holy Trinity, Father, Son and Holy Spirit, I adore Thee profoundly. I offer Thee the most precious Body and Blood, Soul and Divinity of Jesus Christ, present in all the tabernacles of the world . . ."

Finally the angel arose, took the Host and the chalice and gave the children Communion[1] while saying: *"Take the body and blood of Jesus Christ horribly insulted by ungrateful men. Make reparation for their crimes and console your God."*

Then the angel vanished.

Subsequently the Virgin* appeared to the children. She extended her hands from which rays of light streamed upon them and they felt "lost in God." At that moment the crowd heard them cry out: *"O most Blessed Trinity, I adore You! My God, My God, I love You in the most Blessed Sacrament."*

Five other times the Virgin appeared to the children. She told them that men must change their ungodly ways of living or World War I would be followed by World War II and that even "further wars" and "annihilation of whole nations" would

---

[1] One child was communicated with the Host, the other two from the chalice. The 9-year-old boy did not understand and when his 10-year-old cousin explained, he said: "I knew God had entered into me, but I didn't know how."

This statuary group stands on the spot where the three children saw the Angel.

These are actual photographs taken during the miracle which had been foretold at Fatima by the children.

The Miracle itself could not be photographed because of its brilliance.

Even for an eclipse of the sun, photographers use special equipment and "setup" in advance. Yet this was a phenomenon more brilliant than an eclipse. Photographs of the crowd seem as though taken at high noon. The light was visible thirty miles away, and appeared as a great red flash sixteen miles down in Leiria (where the angle of view was such that the climax of the Miracle, the "falling", was not seen.)

The colors have been characterized as "monochromatic sectors" which appeared to revolve and to subsist without any known support. In other words, the colors were not prismatic, but individual rays of brilliant color.

follow the provocations of international Communism. (This was in 1917 when the children in this remote Portuguese hamlet had never heard of Communism and Russia was not considered a threat to the world at large, by anybody anywhere). She ended by saying that the revelation was from God, and that a public miracle would occur on October 13th to prove it.

As far as we know, this is *the only occasion in history when the exact time and place of a public miracle was predicted "so that everyone may believe"*.

That miracle, a phenomenon described by some one hundred thousand witnesses as something like the sun falling toward earth, was seen over a radius of thirty miles. All who saw it thought they were about to die. No natural explanation was found.[1]

When we ask what the miracle proves, what *"everyone may believe"* . . . we are left with the whole revelation of Fatima which began with an apparition of the Eucharist before which an archangel fell in adoration, an exclamation of adoration to God in the Eucharist, a message of reparation practiced through devotion to the Immaculate Heart,* and some remarkable prophecies: World

[1] Many of the witnesses of the "miracle of the sun" are still living. The historic facts can be verified by anybody who is interested. The present writer interviewed hundreds of the witnesses and wrote a book from the testimony given by scientists, journalists, photographers, priests, and even by persons who up to the time of the miracle were atheists. (MEET THE WITNESSES, AMI PRESS, 1961)

War II, the spread of atheistic communism through the entire world, further war, even annihilation of entire nations. Many of these prophecies made in 1917 came true, and the others appeared imminent before the world celebrated the Golden Jubilee of the apparitions in 1967. But in addition to the dire prophecies were two great promises (if the message of Fatima is heeded) :

"Russia will be converted, and *an era of peace will be granted to all mankind.*"

It is remarkable that in 1967 His Holiness, Athenagoras I, Patriarch of the Orthodox,* the religion which is predominant in Russia, said: "I often see a beautiful hand holding the chalice of Our Lord over a nearby hill, and I hear secret voices that speak of love between humanity and peace among men." And on April 22, 1967, the forty-two-year-old daughter of Stalin arrived in the United States for "self-expression" denied to her so long in Russia. She said: "It was impossible to live without God . . ." and from that moment of her belief in Him "the main dogmas of Communism lost their significance for me." There were "no longer capitalists or communists . . . only people, the same everywhere in their hopes and ideals."

In a series of television programs which the present writer produced on the possibility of the conversion of Russia, he interviewed a former captain of Soviet Intelligence who testified that not only was

personal belief in God becoming common in Russia
but that it often reached points of moral heroism.
George F. Kennan, former U. S. Ambassador to
Russia who helped Stalin's daughter come to the
U. S., appealed to Americans to welcome her and
to recognize that "a new era is dawning." At Fatima,
in Portugal, the Blue Army of Our Lady, primarily
through its some five million U. S. members, built a
Russian church near the place of the apparitions
as a gesture of welcome to the great people of the
East. Here every day the Eucharistic Liturgy is celebrated in the same manner as in Russia. The Blessed
Sacrament is reserved in this Russian Church and
simultaneously in a Latin Church just beneath it.
Perhaps history will judge the modern story of Christ
with us, in the Blessed Sacrament, in a light similar
to that of the first centuries from which came the
great era of Middle-Ages-faith that bore the fruit
of modern progress. The triumph of East-West union, after forty years of persecution and literally millions of martyrs (far more than in all the first centuries of Christianity) may well bring the greatest
age of man, greater than most would even dare to
dream. (See FATIMA, page 287.)

Logically enough, we may ask why God seems
to concentrate so much of His miraculous activity
in certain places, such as Fatima and Lourdes. We
cannot read His mind, but we can speculate. Perhaps this concentration is a means of calling men's

attention and allowing proof to build up, as it were, under proper and objective observation. The secular press gives them little space, but it does not and cannot fail to report them when they gradually come to world attention. Miracles can be ignored only when they are isolated occurrences.

However, other Eucharistic miracles occur constantly all over the world. After all, it is the same Christ in the Eucharist whether He be in Lourdes or Alaska, in Fatima or Finland.

We need not believe in any one of them. On the face of it, some seem credible; others seem like pious fables which appeal, we think, only to simple folk. But on second thought, aren't all miracles a sort of baby-talk that God uses to reach us, His childish earthlings, we who strut about pretending to be so grownup, so independent, and so sophisticated and self-reliant?

There is a story told about St. Louis of France. Once he was working in his study when a courtier burst in exclaiming: "Sire, come quickly! Come to the chapel! The Infant Jesus is appearing in the Host in the monstrance."

The saint did not move. "I could not believe more firmly in Christ's presence in the Eucharist if I were to see a miracle," he answered and went back to his writing.

But few men are like St. Louis.

Maybe it is a fable, but there is a strange miracle (though not a cure this time) reputed to have happened just a short distance from Fatima in the town of Santarem. It recalls the bleeding Host held by the angel at Fatima.

When a woman received Communion, she took the Host from her mouth and wrapped it in her handkerchief. And as she was leaving the church somebody approached her and asked: "Are you hurt? Can I help you?"

Blood was dripping through the cloth and seemed to the concerned questioner to be coming from the woman's hand or arm. Actually, it came from the Host she held.

Terrified, the woman ran home leaving a trail of blood behind her. Then she hid the gory mass in a sort of footlocker or blanket chest. That night a light shone around the chest. The woman had no alternative; she had to tell her husband what had happened.

Terrified himself, he called the priest.

To commemorate the event, and also as an act of reparation for the indignity that the woman had visited upon Christ in the Eucharist, the people of Santarem built a special church known simply as "The Church of the Miracle." It enshrines the blood-veined Flesh which to this day is revered.

To attend Mass in that Church of the Miracle

and to see the Flesh displayed in the monstrance above the tabernacle can be a rather disconcerting experience. One person reports:

"When the acolyte rang the sanctuary bell to announce the Consecration* and I heard the familiar words: "This is My Body," I scarcely dared to look. But when I did, I had a distinct feeling of relief: the priest as always was holding up the round Host which still looked like bread. And it seemed a greater, far more wonderful miracle."

Perhaps the reason that the Church pays so little attention to miracles like the one claimed in Santarem is that the daily Eucharistic miracle itself is so stupendous that by comparison the other miracles hardly seem strange or wonderful at all. In any case, the Church does minimize the strange happenings which appear miraculous. Santarem's event, for example, is not so much as mentioned in the Catholic Encyclopedia. If one goes to Santarem he probably will have grave difficulty even to find the church.

The Santarem story is told here in detail, rather than another of many similar instances, because an episcopal investigation was made within hours of the first report, and the Host has been used for benediction and has remained in the custody of the Diocese of Santarem ever since.

That such a story should have been fabricated by the woman and her husband is unlikely because

The "Church of the Miracle", where the Host is reserved. Above, a priest holds the "Host" of Santarem, incorrupt after seven centuries.

it was detrimental to their reputation. That the episcopal commission could have been duped, or collusive in a fraud, is also unlikely. Santarem is too small a city for such a possible fraud, and no effort was made to exploit the event. To the contrary, the diocese went to the expense of building a small church and to this day the event has been little publicized beyond the immediate area. [1] The present ecclesiastical attitude to the "miracle" in Santarem itself could be described as little more than reverent.

Yet stories of divine manifestation keep cropping up, and though many of them may well be fantasy, not all of them are or could be.

There are *many* stories of miracles connected with some outrage against the Blessed Sacrament. To list just a few places where, and times when, such miracles were said to occur: There was Slavings, Moravia in 1120; the little town of Excelles on the border of France and Italy in 1453; Poznan, Poland, in 1599; Breslau, Germany, in 1831; Orthez in the Upper Pyrenees in 1845, and many, many others.

A recent story of profanation of the Blessed Sacrament and Christ's dramatic manifestation was published a few years ago in the Montreal weekly, PATRIE. The event took place in Bui Chu, China.

Most Eucharistic minded persons (frequent

[1] The author knows of no book in which the "Miracle of Santarem" is detailed and he might not have learned of it at all were it not that he lived for a short time in Portugal.

communicants) tend to regret such miracles on the periphery of the major miracle of transubstantiation. They admit that in some instances miracles have been necessary because of blasphemy, lack of faith, or need of reparation. But they rarely express interest in hearing about them. And that seems to be pretty generally the official Church attitude.

The miracle of Bolsena-Orvieto is a notable exception because the Pope personally conducted the investigation almost "on the spot" and thereupon commissioned Saint Thomas Aquinas to write the Mass of the "Body of Christ" (Corpus Christi), for a new feast in the church. The first time a Pope ever traveled in a helicopter was in August of 1964 when Pope Paul flew from the Vatican to Orvieto for the anniversary of the miracle. And even one of the famous "Seven Altars" of Saint Peter's Basilica in Rome commemorates the somewhat gory episode.

The story concerns a man known as Peter of Prague, a Bohemian priest of the 13th century who supposedly doubted the Real Presence. While celebrating Mass at St. Christiana's tomb in the lake town of Bolsena, Italy, he broke the Host after the Consecration and was stunned to see blood flowing from it and dripping onto the corporal (or the square of linen on which the Host and the chalice are placed during Mass) and onto the marble beneath.

Later the corporal was taken to the Cathedral of Orvieto, where to this day it is preserved.

Pope Paul VI celebrates Mass in Orvieto Cathedral where the corporal from Bolsena is reserved.

The corporal from Bolsena, now reserved in the Cathedral of Orvieto. The red
stains have somewhat faded with age and
the corporal is opened to view only on rare
occasions.

Another strange story concerns a citizen of the United States, Frances Allen, daughter of Ethan Allen, the patriot and soldier of the American Revolution. When she was twenty-one she persuaded her mother and stepfather to send her from her home in Vermont to Montreal where she could complete her education at the convent school of the Sisters of the Congregation of Notre Dame.

Once there she soon made herself *persona non grata,* for she took every occasion to mock the Eucharist. For the sake of peace and harmony among the students the Mother Superior decided to ask the girl to leave. One of the nuns, however, begged the Superior to give Frances another chance.

It was of no avail. So for a second time it was decided to send her home.

On the afternoon of her departure she happened to be helping one of the nuns arrange some flowers for the chapel. On impulse the Sister turned to Frances and said: "Would you mind taking them in for me and putting them on the altar?" Then she added, again on impulse: "Be sure to adore the Lord while you are there."

The girl reached the sanctuary gate just a few steps from the altar and suddenly found herself unable to move farther. Her legs seemed paralyzed.

A moment later she fell to her knees babbling words of faith.

The following year she entered the cloister of

Hotel Dieu in Montreal as a postulant, and later she went on to become the first nun from the thirteen original colonies.

Perhaps emotion rather than the direct intervention of God caused a seeming paralysis, but in view of the outcome isn't it logical to suppose that God may well have had a hand in what happened?

This incident occurred back in the early 1800's.

There are similar happenings in our own day. Sr. Mary Claude of the Holy Cross[1] (who wrote of this herself for the present writer) had gone with another sister to visit a sick parishioner. By mistake they called at the wrong house. However the woman who greeted them at the door invited them in and began to ask questions about the faith. Finally, she asked if she could have formal instructions. In the weeks that followed she accepted the doctrine of Christianity eagerly, with one exception: She could not bring herself to believe in the Eucharist.

The Sisters suggested that she attend Benediction of the Blessed Sacrament and they recommended: "When the Host is held up in the monstrance,* ask God to help you to believe in the Real Presence."

The following week the Sisters visited their protege again and inquired how she had liked the ceremony of Benediction.*

"He was beautiful!" came the instant and glowing response.

[1] Member of the Congregation of the Holy Cross, Montreal (1967).

Nonplussed, the Sisters began asking questions, and the neophyte explained that she had seen the Lord leave the monstrance to bless the people and then go back again when the priest returned to the altar. "I saw His wounded side through His pure white garment and the marks of the nails on His hands and feet," she added, and was surprised to know that her experience had been unusual.

Imagination? Possibly. But to the day of her death some years afterward the woman stuck to her story, and she refused to be satisfied with any picture of Christ that she saw. "He was much more beautiful than that," she insisted.

But this book is not meant to be a recital of the unusual or the quaint or the fantastic. Aside from the cures of Lourdes and Fatima, little scientific effort has been made to verify any of the so called miracles, so we cannot speak of them with much assurance. However every Christian knows that the most important Eucharistic miracles are not miracles at all in the sense that they can be outwardly perceived. In the Eucharist this morning Christ enabled a man to overcome his unruly passions; He strengthened a woman against the undertow of her malicious resentment; He calmed a storm of hatred and healed a soul in grief. Miracles of this type happen every day, everywhere, and they are the important miracles of the Eucharist.

Here we have Christ dwelling among us; and

"power goes forth from Him". What was a secret of early Christians becomes a secret of personal force, now, everywhere.

That is perhaps the lasting and most exciting impression we get of the Eucharistic Christ, the effects of the "forces" that are His Body suspended in relation to those of bread: *Power*. One need only experience it for a moment, or see it as Doctor Carrel did, and the whole world changes. No longer are we alone. No longer does life seem meaningless. No longer do crosses weigh. No longer is there room for anything but surging, glorious hope!

CHAPTER XIII

THE SECRET MADE PERSONAL

NOTHING IN THE catacombs cries more eloquently from the past than an inscription written on the tomb of Tarcisius: "Carrying the sacraments of Christ, he chose rather to suffer death *than to betray the heavenly Body* to raging dogs."

That inscription and a boy's skeleton were all that remained to tell the modern world, when the archeologists found them, of a faith in the Eucharist and a heroism that makes fifteen hundred years of united faith in the Eucharist understandable.

We can easily re-create what happened.

In those early centuries, Christians had to assemble in stealth to celebrate the Eucharistic Liturgy. And between celebrations the Eucharist was carried to the sick, to the imprisoned, to those about to face martyrdom, to those in hiding. Tarcisius had the Blessed Sacrament on his person. He was probably taking it to someone in prison, or perhaps even caught in the act of approaching a Christian soon to be put to death. He was seized and beaten to reveal the Christian Secret.

185

What was it he was carrying? Why was he coming to see a Christian who looked forward to receiving him so eagerly that it was evident that he carried something important, something that gave him away?

Rather than permit that they should know, and therefore perhaps dishonor Our Lord in the Blessed Sacrament, Tarcisius let them beat him to death. And all they found was what looked like a piece of bread . . .

"This is the bread which cometh down from Heaven," Our Lord had taught them (John 6,50). Tarcisius had never seen Christ. He had never seen the miracle of the loaves and fishes or the resurrection of Lazarus, or perhaps even the glorified Christ Himself. He died almost two hundred years after the Last Supper. So where did he get such faith out of a world of secrecy and persecution?

Again, we do not have to study back two thousand years. We have the evidence in persons all about us.

To write this one chapter, the writer scanned the biographies of more than a hundred canonized saints*. Each book, without exception, proved to have two chapters: One on the saint's "outstanding" or "heroic" or "unique" devotion to the Eucharist; the other on "special" devotion to the Blessed Virgin. And most of the chapters were written in such a way that the author seemed to feel that these devotions were the *distinguishing* characteristics of the person of whom he was writing.

It is safe to say that there is not a single canonized saint* who has not shown special devotion to the Eucharist, even though some saints manifested the devotion more markedly and obviously than others. We can call them Eucharistic saints (though the term is a bit misleading), or saints who were very particularly devoted to Christ in the Eucharist.

To describe all the Eucharistic saints would take hundreds of pages and but a few examples will do.

St. John Chrysostom, Bishop of Constantinople, lived back in the 4th century when Christianity was first daring to break its three and a half centuries of stark secrecy, a thousand years before the Reformation.

In his homily #50 on the subject of the Eucharist he writes: "Believe therefore that now the same supper is being celebrated as that one at which He presided. This one is no different from that one. And when you see the priest who stretches out (his hand) to you, do not think it is the priest doing it, but the hand of Christ Himself."

One of the saint's homilies of the Gospel of St. Matthew,# 82, is dedicated to the Last Supper. To those who ask why Christ instituted the Blessed Sacrament during the feast of the Pasch he replied that the events of the Old Testament, of which the Pasch was one, were only shadows and figures of that mystery. He established the reality where the image alone had been.

Then he argues that whereas Christ's word cannot err, our senses can and do easily err. Explaining about the bread and wine of the Eucharist, he writes that if we had not been created bodies, He would not use material things to transmit His graces. But "since the soul is united to the body, He gives you spiritual graces by means of sensible things."

In preparing for Communion, says the great Bishop, strive to "be purer than the rays of the sun", and "think what an honor has been given you, what a banquet you have on hand! That what the angels dread to look on, nor gaze at without fear for the splendor which It emits, such is the food with which we are nourished, with which we mingle ourselves, and for which we are made one body and one flesh with Christ."

As Jesus was born of the same substance as ourselves and entered into our nature, thus did He come to all of us, but He likewise comes to each of us separately and in particular. St. John put it this way: "Jesus unites Himself to each one of the faithful, and He with Himself nourishes them and does not trust them to others. In this manner He proves that He has received your flesh."

Then leaping over the centuries we can choose a modern example: Blessed   John Neumann, Bishop of Philadelphia.

Loving his Eucharistic Lord and wishing to dramatize the Blessed Sacrament and to center spiritual life in his diocese around Him, he dreamed of bringing the Forty Hours Devotion[1] to the United States.

At first the idea was received coldly. People on all sides told him: "You can't do that! If you left the Blessed Sacrament exposed in churches for forty long hours, don't you know what would happen? The ignorant and the impious would profane and dishonor It."

The idea might have died there except for what happened one night. The Bishop had been writing letters for hours and he grew so weary that he fell asleep at his desk. When he awoke an hour or so later his papers were a charred mass. Whether a puff of wind had blown a letter into the flames of a candle, or whether the candle had overturned, he could not tell. Only one letter remained intact, except for charred edges. Picking it up he saw that it was the only letter he had written that evening about the Forty Hour Devotion.

At this discovery he dropped to his knees. It seemed to him that a voice was telling him: "As this

[1] During Forty Hours Devotion the Blessed Sacrament is "exposed" or exhibited in the monstrance on the altar for forty consecutive hours (that being the approximate time that Christ lay in the tomb) while continuous adoration is maintained by relays of devout people. Usually the practice is taken up by one church in a diocese after another, so that the "exposition" is continuous if possible within a diocese.

writing was saved from the flames, so shall I preserve
My Son, present in the Blessed Sacrament, from profanation and dishonor. Wait no longer. Carry out
your plan."

The Bishop again eagerly took up his pen. Letter after letter he wrote on through the night, order-
ing the celebration of the Forty Hours Devotion in
every church of his Philadelphia Diocese. The custom spread and today the devotion is practiced
throughout the entire United States.

Having almost at random chosen two Saint
Johns who are centuries apart, may we now turn to
two Thomases?

The great 13th Century philosopher and theologian, St. Thomas Aquinas, has sometimes been
called the Eucharistic Doctor, for he is known not
only for his monumental theological work on the
Eucharist in SUMMA THEOLOGICA but also
for incomparably beautiful hymns to the Blessed Sacrament. It was he who was chosen to write the
Proper parts of the Mass and the Office (or official
prayers) for the feast of Corpus Christi, the feast
on which we honor the Body of the Lord and celebrate, as on Maundy* Thursday, the institution of
the Blessed Sacrament.

The learned doctor used to go to Christ in the
Blessed Sacrament whenever he had a special problem. On his deathbed he made a profession of faith
which should be recorded whenever the Blessed Sac-

rament is discussed. He who is bracketed with Aristotle and Plato as one of the greatest philosophers of all time said just before he died: "If in this world there be any knowledge of this mystery keener than that of Faith, I wish now to affirm that I believe in the Real Presence of Jesus Christ in this Sacrament, truly God and truly man, the Son of God, the Son of the Virgin Mary. This I believe and hold for true and certain."

The second Thomas we chose is Saint Thomas More. When he was Chancellor of England some of his friends reproached him for going to Communion so often. With all his duties and responsibilities they thought that this piety took up too much of his time. He answered their objections with these words: "Your reasons for wanting me to stay away from Holy Communion are exactly the ones which cause me to go so often. My distractions are great, but it is in Communion that I recollect myself. I have temptations many times a day; by daily Communion I get the strength to overcome them. I have much very important business to handle and I need light and wisdom; it is for this very reason that I go to Holy Communion every day to consult Jesus about them."

Now, let us choose two men named Francis. We can begin with St. Francis Assisi. Even when as a young man he was more interested in feats of chivalry than in spiritual matters, his devotion to Christ in the Blessed Sacrament led him to send expensive chalices to poor priests. Later, when he turned from worldliness, his Eucharistic devotion grew. Christ had spoken to Francis from a crucifix and said: "Mend My Church," so the young gallant, with scarcely a backward glance at the old life, rushed off to restore the literally crumbling parish church of St. Damian. He begged enough oil for it to keep a light burning night and day before the Blessed Sacrament. Soon afterwards, God called Francis to found His Order of friars, which today we call the Franciscans.

As the leader of his little group of men, Francis wrote letters giving advice and instructions.

Five of eight letters of Francis of Assisi which have come down to us treat of the Blessed Sacrament, either entirely or in part. In one of them he exhorts the clergy: "Keep churches clean, altars and everything belonging to the celebration of Mass and the administration of the Sacraments . . . how wretched are the chalices, corporals* or other linens where the Body and Blood of Our Lord Jesus Christ is sacrificed . . . Our Lord is loving enough to entrust Himself to our hands and we handle Him and receive Him on our lips day after day."

He taught his friars that whenever they saw a church they should bow low to salute the Presence inside, and whenever the Blessed Sacrament was being carried anywhere, he added: "Let all the people on bended knee render praise, honor and glory to the Lord God, living and true."

In yet another letter he said: "Let everything in man halt in awe, let all the world quake and let heaven exult when Christ the Son of the living God is there on the altar in the hands of the priest."

Then he writes: "In this world I see nothing bodily of the most high Son of God except His most holy Body and Blood," and he reminded his priests to preach the reception of the Sacrament. Meanwhile *he himself would never become a priest because he did not feel worthy of such a high state.*

Often he speaks of the reverence in which priests should be held, even bad ones. After all, he says, "their hands have touched the Lord". He deemed no dignity greater than that of the priesthood, "because of its sublime privilege of consecrating the Body and Blood of Christ."

To priests themselves he urged dedication and devotion because they are "chosen by the great King to bring to the nations of the earth what they themselves have learned and gathered, especially before the tabernacle."

His own devotion to the Real Presence was extraordinary and his first biographer, Thomas de Celano, writes: "Every fiber of the heart of Francis was aglow with love for the Sacrament of the Body of Christ."

One could go on and on about Francis of Assisi,

but we turn again to another Francis, separated by centuries of time: St. Francis de Sales. This gentle, courteous French Bishop is described as "one of the finest bishops and most attractive men that Christianity has ever produced."[1]

In his book *Introduction to a Devout Life* he writes: "When you have received It (the Host) excite your heart to come and render homage to this King of salvation; speak to Him of your most intimate affairs; contemplate Him within you where He has come for your happiness; finally give Him the best welcome possible and behave in such a manner that by all your acts it may be known that God is with you."

Of frequent Communion he said: "If worldly folk ask you why you communicate so often, say it is in order to learn to love God, to purge yourself of your imperfections, to free yourself from your miseries, to console yourself in your afflictions, to support yourself in your weaknesses. Say that there are two kinds of people who should communicate often: the perfect, because being so well-disposed, they would do great wrong if they did not approach the Source and Fountain of Perfection, and the imperfect with the end of being reasonably able to aspire to perfection; the strong, that they may not become weak, and the weak to become strong; the sick that they may be cured, and the healthy that they

[1] Dictionary of Saints.

may not fall sick; and that you, imperfect, weak and sick, need to communicate often with Him Who is your perfection, your strength and your doctor . . . *Say that you receive the Holy Sacrament in order to learn how to receive it,* for one never does well that in which one has not had practice."

However, does such stress on the Eucharist in the lives of holy persons imply that the Eucharist is the one means of Grace and the only mark of Christian heroes? No, because if this were true the only Christian saints would be those who have access to the Eucharist. And Christ did not promise to say: "Possess the kingdom, for you have received Communion often." Rather He will say "Possess the kingdom . . . for I was hungry and you gave Me to eat; I was thirsty, and you gave Me to drink . . ."

But during twenty centuries of Christian history we find greatest devotion to the Eucharist in those who did feed the hungry heroically, those who visited the imprisoned, those who gave their own lives to save others, those who truly loved their fellow men as Christ taught. And this is so universally true, of those Christlike persons who had access to the Blessed Sacrament, that almost any of them might be singled out for *exceptional* love of Christ in the Sacrament of His Love.

Pope Leo XIII remarked of St. Paschal Baylon: "Of all the saints who have been known for their extraordinary devotion to the Most Blessed Sacrament, St. Paschal occupies first place." In his Apostolic letter *Providentissimus Deus,* Leo declared St. Paschal the patron of Eucharistic Congresses* and associations. But what about St. Peter Julian, St. John Eudes, etc., etc.? It almost seems that Pope Leo had chosen at random.

We have not yet mentioned women who were outstanding Christians.

One of the most famous was Catherine of Siena. Known principally for her ambassadorial missions and her part in persuading the Pope to return from Avignon to Rome, she deserves rather to be known for her exceptional devotion to the Eucharist. It was closeness to Christ in the Eucharist which made all her feats possible.

Then again leaping the centuries we come to Elizabeth Bayley Seton of the United States who as a young Episcopalian widow visiting Italy attended Mass with Italian friends and heard an Englishman mutter at the Elevation of the Host, "This is what they call their Real Presence." She was deeply disturbed by the remark and later wrote in her diary of the "unfeeling interruption".

Shortly afterward she wrote her sister-in-law: "How happy we would be if we believed what these dear souls believe, that they possess God in the Sacrament and that He remains in their churches and is carried to them when they are sick! Oh, my! When they carry the Blessed Sacrament under my windows, while I feel the loneliness and sadness of my case, I cannot stop my tears at the thought: My God, how happy I would be, even so far away from all so dear, if I could find You in the Church as they do . . . The other day, in a moment of excessive distress, I fell on my knees without thinking when the Blessed Sacrament passed by and cried in an agony to God to bless me if He was there, that my whole soul desired only Him."

When she returned to New York she attended her own church as usual, but chose a side pew which faced the Catholic church opposite. She records that she constantly found herself speaking to the Blessed Sacrament there.

Later she burned with faith at no time more strongly than when she was about to receive Communion.

She wrote: "God is everywhere, in the very air I breathe, yes everywhere, but in His Sacrament of the Altar He is as present actually and really as my soul within my body; in His Sacrifice daily offered as really as once offered on the Cross."

On New Year's Day, 1821, Mother Seton was near death. To receive communion in those days one had to abstain from food and drink from midnight, and when a nurse requested the dying saint to take a beverage she said: "Never mind the drink. One Communion more and then eternity." Thus in the face of death she reminded us that only on this earth is Eucharistic union with Christ possible . . . an honor even the angels cannot enjoy.

It is a union not to be compared to the beatific vision, but it has the merit of being voluntary. To see God is to love Him, but the average person who receives the Eucharist sees nothing but the appearances of bread and wine.

Women who have become Eucharistic saints are like the stars, innumerable. Some of them lived miraculously on no other food but the Eucharist. St. Catherine of Siena whom we just mentioned was one who lived for months on the Eucharist alone. St. Angela of Foligno was another, and in her case this miraculous state lasted twelve years. In our own day, Alexandrina who died in 1955 lived for 167 months with the Eucharist as her sole food.★

Who can doubt the promise made nearly two thousand years ago: "Behold I am with you all days even to the consummation of the world"? Aren't those who cannot believe prompted to cry out like Mrs. Seton: "Jesus, bless me if You are really there, for my whole soul desires only You!"?

In our introduction to this book we remarked that because it is for everyone, it cannot satisfy everyone: "It will seem too skimpy for the professional." And perhaps this is nowhere more evident than in the chapter on proofs (or miracles) and in this

★ Alexandrina was hospitalized and closely watched day and night for forty days at a stretch by doctors and nurses. Her subsistence solely on the Eucharist was certified as scientifically inexplicable. Her mission paralleled that of the apparitions of Fatima. She died October 13th, 1955. Her last words: "Do not sin. The pleasures of this life are worth nothing. This sums up everything. Say the Rosary every day."

chapter. Well over a hundred miracles were prepared. Only three were used. In the end the truth of one miracle should be as strong as that of a hundred, and the example of one saint should be as compelling as those of a hundred.

But there is one miracle and one final example of a completely Eucharistic life which we feel compelled to include.

High up in the mountains just to the north of Beirut is the dead body of a priest which exudes what seems to be a mixture of blood and water. When his tomb is opened each year, the body actually is floating in the liquid which in twelve months has accrued to a depth of about three inches. The body itself, as described in an official doctor's report witnessed by this writer, is as though it had been dead only a few days. Miracles performed at the tomb are so startling and so numerous that they remind one of the miracles of Lourdes.

We ourselves visited there in the spring of 1967 to examine the evidence and talk with witnesses. It was our conclusion, after journeys around the world and more than fifty trips to Europe, that this was perhaps the greatest single phenomenon of our time.

One of the unusual aspects of this phenomenon is the very fact that this priest, on a mountain almost 5,000 feet straight up from the sea, was never heard of at all in the outside world during his life. He was a Maronite monk whose life was his daily Mass.

Near the Monastery was a hermitage where the monks could go for several days of quiet retreat. It had no heat, very small cells, and a tiny chapel. This priest asked frequently to spend days at the hermitage and finally obtained permission to remain there constantly for twenty-three years. Other priests took turns sharing the hermitage with him. They never recorded anything very extraordinary except that he chose to say his Mass about eleven o'clock in the morning so that he could have all the morning to prepare for the Mass, and then have the rest of the day for thanksgiving. And at the elevation of the Host, since he was of Oriental rite, he had permission to add the words: "O most Holy Trinity, receive Thy Divine Son for the conversion of sinners!"

It was while he held the Host elevated, his heart speaking this prayer, that he collapsed at the altar in 1898. A priest assisting at the Mass had to pry the Blessed Sacrament from the saintly man's clenched fingers. Eight days later, after suffering which seemed to be a perpetuation of that moment of Calvary, he died on the bare floor in a room behind the chapel.

Like all the other monks, he was buried in the general cemetery. It was to be expected that he would soon be forgotten. But a light was seen around the tomb. Finally in 1950 the monks asked permission to have the body exhumed.

During the subsequent years the body has been

exhumed and buried several times until finally a part of the old monastery was set aside where the tomb is now above ground. Previously, although the body remained absolutely incorrupt and constantly exuded liquid, the very coffins themselves disintegrated. Even the bottom of an exterior zinc coffin split beneath the feet of the body. Attestations of the various doctors which were placed in the tomb after each examination remained intact. The very paper, which normally would have yellowed, remained fresh even though iron boxes in which these attestations were placed disintegrated.

The Monastery began to keep records of miracles performed through the intercession of this priest from 1950 onward. Within two years they recorded over twelve hundred.

Obviously God had a special reason for performing miracles to call the attention of the world to this obscure priest of the mountain whose whole life centered in and around the Eucharistic Liturgy.

Pope Paul VI declared him blessed on May 12, 1965, prior to the final session of the Ecumenical Council. His body had been exhumed and found incorrupt for the first time only fifteen years before. He is now Blessed Charbel Makhlouf*.

The miracle of Blessed Charbel reminds the world of the center of this man's entire life: the Eucharist. It is noteworthy that he stands at the bridge of the world between the East and the West, himself of an Eastern rite and Semitic race, in that part of Asia where the East and the West truly meet. The actual prayer which Father Charbel recited at the time of the elevation probably was longer than given above but it is as Father Ciade quoted: "The essence of Blessed Charbel's thought . . . the offering of the Eucharist to the Trinity for sinners."

CHAPTER XIV

MOTHER OF THE SECRET

As we draw near the end of this very much condensed version of the most dramatic and repercussive belief in history, the writer dares to intrude a personal reaction as a prelude to what must now follow.

Many amazing things came to light during the seven years of this book's preparation, but to the writer the most amazing of all was the frequency of a symbol around the tomb of Saint Peter that was rarely mentioned and is little known. The greatest expert on the *graffiti* around Peter's tomb says that this one frequently repeated symbol was usually found in conjunction with the symbols of Christ and the Eucharist.

It was the symbol of the Virgin Mary.

And this is surprising because there is hardly any mention of her in the gospel. True, she had remained behind after the Ascension and was perhaps the centre of the new Church on the stunning day of Pentecost. And she must have meant a great deal to the early Christians because of her intimacy with Christ and because He performed His first miracle (the one which prefigured the Eucharist) at her request: It was the transformation of water into wine at the marriage at Cana. And He performed that first miracle even though He said that His time had not yet come.

But it must be evident that if we could speak of "Eucharistic Saints", as we did in the last chapter, beginning with the boy-martyr, Tarcisius, then the Blessed Virgin must be explained as the Eucharistic Saint *par excellence*.

This attitude of the early Christians is borne out by the inscription on the tomb of Abercius found in Hieropolis in Asia Minor: "Faith everywhere led me forward and everywhere provided as my food a fish of exceeding great size and perfection which a Holy Virgin drew with her hands from a fountain and ever gives this to its friends to eat, wine of great virtue, mingled with bread . . ."

From the whole inscription it is certain that the fish is used acrostically and means "Jesus Christ, Son of God, Saviour". The fountain is the Church. And of the conclusion there can be no doubt: the Holy Virgin gives the Eucharist.

Even today few Christians would place this much emphasis on the Blessed Virgin in relation to the world's greatest secret.

Apparently something, over the centuries, has been lost . . . something that was contained almost entirely and exclusively in tradition (see page 80-81).

At first glance, she may not seem a Eucharistic

saint at all. Her role in God's plan is closely bound up with other mysteries of Faith, notably the Incarnation. Yet she is THE Eucharistic saint above all others for one big reason: she gave the Lord a body. It was she who gave Him flesh and blood, the very same flesh and blood which comes to us in the Sacrament. She can truly be called "the Mother of the Eucharist."

Since the embryo she conceived was of the Holy Spirit, she, as no other mother of the human race, could say as she held her Infant in her arms: *"This is my body."*

Saint Peter Julian Eymard, through whose intercession have occurred miracles as great as any recorded in previous pages, called her *Our Lady of the Most Blessed Sacrament**. And Saint Pius X, "The Pope of daily Communion," called this "The most theological of all Mary's titles after that of the Mother of God."

St. Peter Julian's Congregation received the privilege of celebrating a feast on May 13th in honor of Our Lady of the Most Blessed Sacrament. Subsequently, Our Lady appeared at Fatima on this feast as though to verify the title. Rays of light streamed from her hands upon the three children who saw her. Those standing about heard the children suddenly cry out together: "O Most Holy Trinity, I adore Thee! My God, my God, I love Thee in the Most Blessed Sacrament!"

Later the children said that as the light from Mary's hands engulfed them they "felt lost in God" and impelled to cry out in adoration of the Most Blessed Trinity: "My God, my God! I love Thee in the most Blessed Sacrament."

The authenticity of the Fatima vision, as we mentioned previously, was confirmed by a public miracle performed at a predicted time and place and witnessed by some 100,000 persons: *"So that everyone may believe."*

May 13th, Feast of Our Lady of the Most Blessed Sacrament, is now also the Feast of Our Lady of the Rosary of Fatima. In 1967, Pope Paul VI flew to Fatima on this day and prayed in the company of hundreds of thousands for world peace.

It would seem that Pope Paul was anxious to fulfill within his own lifetime the great and consoling prophesy of St. John Bosco* that following an Ecumenical Council great storms would arise, but when the Sovereign Pontiff succeeded in anchoring the barque of Peter to the twin columns of devotion to the Blessed Virgin and to the Blessed Sacrament the storms would subside and the great era of unity and peace would follow.

By 1967 Pope Paul had made five historic journeys all related directly to devotion to the Eucharist, to the Blessed Virgin, and to Unity and Peace. He was the first Pope to ride in a helicopter when he flew to Orvieto for the Centennial of the Miracle of the Bleeding Host (see page 174). He was first Pope after Peter to go to the Holy Land and beyond into India to participate in a Eucharistic Congress*. His major Encyclical on the Eucharist is appended to this book, and on the occasion of his pilgrimage to Fatima on May 13, 1967, he issued a major Encyclical on the true meaning of the devotion to the Blessed Virgin whom he had proclaimed during the Ecumenical Council to be "Mother of the Church."

To understand Mary's role better, a diagram might help. Admittedly it is only a slight help for it is only a remote analogy. After all we cannot draw pictures of God.

First God existed alone. We draw Him as a triangle.

Then outside of Himself He created man "in His own image", giving him free will and allowing His light to flow freely to him. We represent man attached to the triangle, full of divine light.

Man, wanting to be equal to God, decided to disobey Him. This sin of futile and prideful defiance must have been the greatest evil of all time, because man in his pristine state of enlightenment was able to see the disruptive horror of the evil more clearly than any man has since been able to do. Also he was closer to God than perhaps any saint (with the exception of Mary) has ever become since, and yet he chose to separate Himself from God. So now we draw him separate from God, separate from his source of light. He was in lonely darkness.

By original sin, man loses grace and is separated from God.

And the Lord God sent him out... to till the earth from which he was taken. Gen. III, 23.

Foreseeing her extraordinary fidelity, God then preserved one member of the human race from the black shadow of the first sin. This preservation and this privilege we call the Immaculate Conception of Mary.* We draw her attached to the triangle, full of light and giving forth light.

One of the human race (Virgin Mary) is preserved free from sin in anticipation of Redemption.

Hail Mary, full of Grace, the Lord is with thee. Luke, I, 28.

Through this immaculate person, faithful to God where Eve had been faithless, the Second Person of the Blessed Trinity was united to human nature. He came on earth and spent thirty-three years enlightening man ("The Light came into the darkness" Ch. I, St. John) and then instituted the Blessed Eucharist to restore more light to man. So now we draw man once again united to God, but inside a new triangle, because God has become man:

Mary conceived by the Holy Ghost, and GOD BECAME MAN, redeemed us, and made possible again our union with God IN HIS OWN PERSON:

"I and the Father are one . . .[1] I came forth from the Father and have come into the world[2] . . . I will send you from the Father the Spirit of truth Who proceeds from the Father . .[3] . . . Abide in Me, and I in you . . .[4] . . . that all may be one, even as Thou, Father in Me and I in Thee; that they may also be one in us . . .[5] (From the discourse of Our Lord on the night He instituted the Holy Eucharist)

[1]John 10, 30; [2]17, 28; [3]17, 26; [4]15-4; [5]17-21.

Though man never did, and never will, recover his first shining clarity of intellect, and though the propensity to sin and concupiscence remains as the result of original sin, God now gives the poor myopic creature greater light and grace than under the Old Dispensation—and He gives it in a special way in the Eucharist. *Instituting the Eucharist, Christ prayed that all might be one as He and the Father are one.*

Mary's role, as we see, began before Christ was born, and we must love her because by bearing Christ she gave back to humanity the hope of salvation that the first mother lost for us. She is really our mother, *the mother of our supernatural life.*

Mary's role also continued through Calvary, and it continued afterward. Indeed, we should use the present tense, for it continues in the Eucharist.

We see that Christ loved her on Calvary and provided for her before He died by placing her in the care of St. John. We love her then, because He did.

Moreover, we love her because He gave her to us through John: "Son, behold thy mother."

Surely also we love her because everything that she did for human souls she did with tremendous generosity. With wholehearted abandon she placed her life and her very being quite simply in God's hands to use as a tool or an instrument as suited His purposes. Whatever He wanted, she wanted with every fiber of mind and heart.

What does God want? What does God always
will? St. Paul tells us succinctly: "This is the will of
God, your sanctification."

Our Lord Himself emphasized this one day
when someone interrupted Him with the announcement that His mother was outside. His love for her
was well known. He had remained alone with her
until He was thirty years of age, and He performed
His first miracle, before His time, at her mere suggestion. Now He profited by this interruption to
show that He loved her not just because she was His
mother, but because *she fulfilled God's will*:

"And who is my mother and who are my brethren?" He asked. "Those who do the will of my
Father."

So Mary by all that she did brought Christ to
the world and to souls. Today *she is still bringing
Christ to the world and to souls, and souls to Christ,
especially to Christ in the Eucharist*. And this is
demonstrable.

We can go to any one of her shrines throughout
the world . . . to Pompeii, Fatima, Lourdes, Pont-
main, to Guadalupe near Mexico City, and so on and
on. In any of these places where she has appeared
and a shrine has been established in her honor *we
find major activity centered on the same reality: the
Mass and the Eucharist*.

So obviously Mary continues to lead man to one Person and to one place: to Christ in the tabernacle.

Strange? Not at all! We have seen that she herself was the first tabernacle. She was the first to carry the body of Christ (though it was not then called the Eucharist) on an errand of mercy when she went to her cousin, Elizabeth. As soon as she entered the house, Elizabeth cried out: "Whence is it that the mother of my Lord should come to me?"

St. Alphonsus asks: "Why does Elizabeth not say, 'Why is it that the Incarnate God comes to me?' Why does she say, 'Why is it that the *mother* . . . comes to me?' "

Alphonsus answers his own question by saying that Elizabeth knew that in welcoming the mother she was welcoming the Son; and the miracle of her own unborn child's presanctification* proved it.

If doubts about the Eucharist sometimes plague our minds, we can think of the tabernacle of the young mother of Nazareth. Is it any more remarkable that Jesus should be in a tabernacle on an altar than that He was in an embryonic state in Mary's womb? Is it any more remarkable that a box-like structure should contain Him than should a microscopic egg?

Just above we spoke of Mary's shrines and her role as guide-to-Christ in these places.

Today this is something that a person need not merely read about, or argue about, or wonder about.

Today anybody can see for himself. How far away
are Lourdes or Fatima? Thanks to modern transpor-
tation facilities these places are only hours away,
and for some people reading these lines, perhaps less
than an hour away, perhaps minutes.

All of these places are filled with crowds who
begin to pray at the spot where the Virgin supposedly appeared, but who end up before the Eucharist.
We repeat that the acts of worship provided at all
these so-called "Marian" shrines are the Eucharistic
sacrifice or the Mass, and the Benediction of the
Blessed Sacrament.

Among the crowds are invalids who arrive
clamoring: "Lord, that I may see!" or "Lord, that
I may walk!" But (despite many miracles) comparatively few of these invalids receive physical help.
Instead, they receive spiritual help. Suddenly, they
are awakened as though from a drugged sleep. Their
spirit soars. They know a new calm, and a joy, and
a peace beyond understanding. Their lives are re-
newed. They feel like different people.

How? Why?

Even the casual observer can see that they have
received an increase of faith and love and an inde-
finable glow which one can only call the light of the
Eucharist.

Yes, that is what a visitor to a Marian shrine
sees in others and experiences himself: light.

It is not the kind of light that we turn on when we flip a switch, but the kind of light which must have shone from the face of Moses when He descended from the mountain after talking with the Lord; Scripture says that his face appeared horned with rays of light. Or it is the kind of light which artists see aureating the face of a holy person and which they portray on their canvases as halos. A person who has never seen such light radiating from another's face has missed one of life's most memorable experiences.

"Oh, if only the sinner in the darkest, blackest night only knew enough to call on Mary!" exclaimed St. Alphonsus. "He would at once find light."

This eminent churchman whose books have helped many a struggling Christian, avers that the whole world would change quickly if enough people would turn to Mary, our prime intercessor with Christ.

Other saints also recognize this role of Mary's. Before Communion St. Therese often pictured herself as a little girl with a soiled face and grimy clothes who ran to her mother asking to be made ready to meet the king.

Of course we too can always go to Mary and ask her to prepare us for Christ. We can do this even if we cannot visit her shrines. After all, few Christians, percentage-wise, ever get to shrines. True,

"Lord, that I may see!"

space is shrinking but that fact does not provide dollars for travel.

Fortunately, there are many ways of reaching Mary, and through her, her Son. St. Louis de Monfort, author of *True Devotion to the Blessed Virgin,* tells us that the best way to adore Christ in the Blessed Sacrament is to place our hearts spiritually in the Immaculate Heart of Mary. In essence, this French saint says that the only *true devotion* to Mary is the one *which relates to Christ* and relates us through her to Him. He advocated devotion to Mary as a sure, easy, safe way to reach union with Christ. Any devotion to Mary for its own sake he labels "false".

Pope Paul VI made this thought the central message of his encyclical *Signum Magnum,* issued on May 13, 1967, when His Holiness went in pilgrimage to Fatima.

A wise and imaginative man who had the same notion expressed it this way: "Have you ever tried to drink water without a glass, or without putting it in a container? It is just as awkward and difficult to try to drink from the fountain of life without using Mary as a vessel." And that this was understood by the early Christians is confirmed by the tablet of Abercius.

Perhaps some of us are inhibited by the feeling that if we pray to Mary we may be taking some honor from God. But when we use the glass as a

Saint Therese of Lisieux, whose autobiography thrilled over two million readers and whose spiritual feats caused Pius XI to call her the star of the Twentieth Century, said that before each Communion she ran to her Mother Mary like a child with soiled and dirty clothes so that she could be quickly made clean and beautiful for the visit of the King of Kings.

drinking vessel so that we won't spill any of the water, do we offend the water?

As we go to Communion we can ask Mary to lend us her immaculate heart in which to receive her Son; we can ask her to adore Him in us and for us and in union with us. Surely Christ, Who comes to us in the Eucharist, will be pleased to find not just sinful, unworthy creatures like ourselves, but at least our awareness and our love for His mother in our hearts.

At first to think of me and Mary and Christ simultaneously seems complicated, like learning to swim. To learn to swim properly we must learn separately how to breathe, how to move the arms and how to move the legs. When we first try to swim we may wonder if we are *ever* going to learn to coordinate the separate functions. Then suddenly the day comes when we roll for breath automatically, arms and legs fall into rhythm, and we are able to enjoy the sheer freedom of motion as we speed almost effortlessly through the water. We have conquered a new element.

So when we first start to pray as St. Louis Grignon teaches us, and as we are instructed to do at Fatima, we may expect to feel slightly awkward.

When some persons first try to swim they may almost drown and be afraid to try again. Others may waste much time envying the swimmers who have mastered the technique but may never really try themselves. But in learning to go to Jesus through Mary we have a constant teacher: Christ. He gave us Mary. He set the example by obeying her Himself for thirty years. He performed His first miracle at her request. He gave her to the whole human race through John on Calvary.

Have we forgotten these truths?

The early Christians had them ever in mind. As we see in recent archeological discoveries in the Mediterranean area, the early Christians frequently engraved in the stone walls of their subterranean havens the *M* along with the *X* and the *P*. The man who wanted to leave a memento of his faith spoke not only of the fish, but of the fish "which a holy Virgin drew with her hands from the fountain and ever gave His friends to eat . . . wine of great virtue mingled with bread."

Is it any surprise that many who rejected Mary's intercession after the sixteenth century, ended up also by rejecting Christ in the Eucharist? And vice versa?

CHAPTER XV

REPARATION

PERHAPS ONE REASON we have radically condensed the material in this book is because we wanted to speed to this moment when we are about to recall a little remembered but most touching fact about the Last Supper during which Christ gave Himself to the world. It was recently illustrated, during a pilgrimage to Jerusalem, in a most graphic way.

A group of pilgrims had climbed Mt. Zion to visit the Cenacle in Jerusalem.

The room was very plain. The Jews with more tolerance than we Christians might show if the holiest place of another religion were over the holiest place of our own, kept the room in repair and open to pilgrims. But the floor was covered with dust.

The priest who headed the group of twenty-one Christians asked them to gather in a circle in the approximate area where Christ washed the apostles' feet, celebrated the Passover and instituted the Eucharist.

"The floor is too dirty for all of us to recline as the apostles did," he said, "but would one of you like to volunteer?"

Then the priest proceeded to recline in the dust himself, and a volunteer, following that lead, did likewise.

"That's right," Father said to his floor companion. "If Christ were in the center of the table you, at His side, would naturally recline in the opposite direction as you have done."

Then addressing the group, the priest went on: "Remember reading in the Gospels about the beloved disciple who reclined at table next to the Master? At one point in the meal he actually rested his head on the Lord's breast. Now as we two men lie here, our heads almost touch. If I slightly shift my position, as I would naturally do in the course of a long meal, it would be easy for the man next to me to rest his head on my chest."

Here he drew the volunteer's head into position to demonstrate.

"That was the first act of devotion to the Sacred Heart of Jesus," he declared.

Suddenly in that room of sacred memories the past sprang to life and became for the moment the pulsing present. The wonder of Christ's Sacred Heart beating with love for man beneath John's head became something that everybody there could almost feel and hear.

How near, how approachable, how lovable Christ is!

John acknowledged Christ as the Master, yet

The room of the Last Supper on Mount Zion in Jerusalem as it is today. Here Christ instituted the Eucharist.

this apostle had dared to inch over and rest his head familiarly upon the Master's heart! John had evidence that Christ was the Miracle-Worker. John had been on Mt. Tabor when Christ, transfigured with dazzling light, had spoken with the prophets Elias and Moses. John had heard the awesome voice from heaven saying: "This is My Beloved Son." Indeed, John had heard Christ say, and had believed the words: "I and the Father are One." Yet this apostle dared such intimacy!

Yes, Christ was lovable and approachable. Every person in that room, gazing at the two men on the floor, was convinced.

But there we were after only a moment, slipping back into the past tense!

Why are we mortals so prone to think of Christ as Someone Who lived in the long ago only? Why can't we always sustain our awareness of how approachable Christ *is?*

The *words* He used centuries ago are for now, as well as for then and for every bit of time. The *things He did* centuries ago are for now as well as for then and for every bit of time. The life He lived centuries ago *He actually lives* in His eternal present at every moment in every tabernacle in the world. Today each of us, by the reception of Communion, *can in effect step into the place of the beloved apostle.* Each of us can rest his head on the Sacred Heart.

Is it any wonder then that in our own time we

should be so forcefully reminded of the Eucharist
as we were in the miracle at Fatima, and previously
in the appearance of Christ . . . coming forth from
the monstrance . . . to Saint Margaret Mary Alacoque* in a little chapel in France?

Is it any wonder, when so many millions of
persons in the world today have refused His loving
invitation to come to Him in the Eucharist that He
appears out of the monstrance to complain?

"Behold the Heart that has so loved men," he
told the saint. "In return: . . . ingratitude . . . contempt in the Sacrament of Love."

Since saints crop up everywhere in these pages
like dandelions in the spring, some readers may well
ask how people who are not saints but who are at least
struggling to keep a foothold on the straight and narrow should express devotion to the Eucharist. Aside
from receiving Communion frequently, which is
paramount, is there any special pious practice that
they can cultivate?

When a certain man asked himself that question
one day, it seemed to him that instantly he had a
clear answer in the Sacred Heart Devotion,* a devotion of reparation to Christ for the indifference
of so many Christians.

At the time, the man was in the little chapel in
Paray-le-Monial, France, where three hundred years
ago Christ stepped from the Eucharist to speak to
the Visitation nun, Sister Margaret Mary. He told

her of the love of His Heart for men and of their indifference to Him, and He asked for comfort and
for reparation.

As this man was conjuring up the scene in his
imagination, an old priest entered the sanctuary
and held up the monstrance with the Host to give
Benediction of the Blessed Sacrament to those in the
Chapel. Then, about to replace the Host in the
tabernacle, he turned to the small knot of worship-
pers in the pews and, with tears in his eyes, said:
"Why, oh why would our Lord have to appear to
ask us to make reparation to Him?"

Why indeed!

The Sacred Heart devotion and devotion to the
Eucharist are logically intertwined. No wonder that
little chapel in Paray-le-Monial, where *formal* devotion to the Sacred Heart began, has become a center
of Eucharistic devotion.

It seems appropriate that here in this same
chapel was given the inspiration for two of the most
dramatic Eucharistic practices of our day: To Emily
Tamisier, a humble laywoman, came the idea of
Eucharistic Congresses;* to Father Mateo came the
idea of the "Enthronement of the Sacred Heart"[1] in
the home, and a chain of a million hours of adoration

---

[1] The Enthronement of the Sacred Heart is the recognition of
the sovereignty of Christ over the Christian family, affirmed
outwardly by a ceremonious, solemn installation of an image
of the Sacred Heart in a place of honor in any home, accompanied by a prescribed prayer of consecration.

Inscription over chapel door here in Paray-le-Monial, France, reads: "In this church Our Lord revealed His Heart to Saint Margaret Mary."

of Christ in the Eucharist around the world.

It was in a Confessional of this chapel that
Margaret Mary first told Father Claude Columbiere:
"When I was kneeling in adoration before the Blessed
Sacrament, suddenly *I saw our Lord come from the
monstrance and stand before the altar*. Through His
robe I saw His heart surrounded by fire and He told
me: 'Behold the heart which has so loved men. It
has spared nothing . . . In return I receive from most
people only ingratitude by irreverence and sacrilege,
by coldness, by contempt for Me and the Sacrament
of Love.' "

After long and exhaustive study, far more detailed perhaps than that of any court trial in which
an accused person's life might be at stake, the Church
finally and officially accepted the apparition as genuine. Over two centuries later, in our own day, the
nun was canonized and the priest beatified.

The Eucharistic Christ Who had stepped from
the monstrance asked Margaret Mary, among other
things, to establish the practice of spending one hour
monthly before the Blessed Sacrament in prayer, the
so-called Holy Hour. From then on she herself kept
prayerful vigil from eleven o'clock to midnight on
the eve of the first Friday of every month. She would
meditate on the desolation that Christ felt when aban-
doned by His apostles, when He suffered excruciating
mental and physical anguish in the Garden of Gethsemane. Thus she prepared in a special way to re-

Left is the tabernacle of the original altar in the chapel of Paray le Monial, surmounted by painting of the vision of Christ coming from the Blessed Sacrament. And here is the new altar, in the same chapel, changed after Vatican Council II to emphasize identity of the Eucharist with sacrifice: The tabernacle has been incorporated into the altar. Previously the priest celebrated the liturgy with his back to the people.

ceive a Communion of reparation on the following morning, the first Friday of the month.

The practice at least of the First Friday Communion (though not always of the Holy Hour) has become very widespread. On that day of the month the churches are filled and the Masses well attended around the entire globe.

After Christ's revelations to St. Margaret Mary, St. Peter Julian founded the Congregation of the Fathers of the Blessed Sacrament and launched the Eucharistic League. The nation of France, in final acknowledgment of St. Margaret Mary's revelation, built the national shrine on the highest hill in Paris, Montmartre, for perpetual adoration of the Eucharist. The white sugar-loaf towers of Sacre Coeur dominate the city. In Rome the practice of the Forty Hours, another Eucharistic devotion, was extended to so many churches that the act of homage to our Lord in the Blessed Sacrament begins in a different church somewhere in the city one right after the other, all year long.

Obviously this close association of the Eucharist with the Sacred Heart Devotion, which developed after the apparitions in Paray-le-Monial, does not imply that only the Heart of Christ is present in the Blessed Sacrament. Clearly "the Heart of Christ" is a metaphorical expression similar to the expression: "I love you with all my heart." In essence, Christ came from the monstrance at Paray-le-Monial

In the Visitation Chapel in Paray, contains the remains of the body of this saint to whom Our Lord revealed His Sacred Heart in "Final appeal for the love of men."

to whisper this to each of us.

Pope Pius XII, whose *Mediator Dei* is considered by some a more precise modern definition of the Eucharist than the decrees of Vatican Council II, also wrote *Haurietis Aquas* (1956) on devotion to the Sacred Heart. A professor of Dogma at the University of Fribourg says: "It should be made required reading for everybody who feels enthusiasm for the liturgy for it is an example of translating a popular devotion into terms of integral Christian piety." [1] But presuming that the average reader is now learning of the Eucharistic liturgy for the first time, we cannot go into the subject in detail.

But why was it ever necessary for Christ to have resorted to such a petty miracle as His appearance to Sister Margaret Mary to reaffirm the greatest love that the world has ever known?

In our survey some objected to the word "petty" to describe the miracle of Christ's appearance out of the Eucharist. By the contrast to the miracle of the Eucharist itself this Appearance (and others like it) is quite small, and it is also a reproach. He said:

"My daughter, I come into your heart. Through your person may you atone for the offenses which I receive from lukewarm and slothful hearts which do not honor Me in the Sacrament."

[1] **Meeting Christ in the Sacraments**, pg. 368.

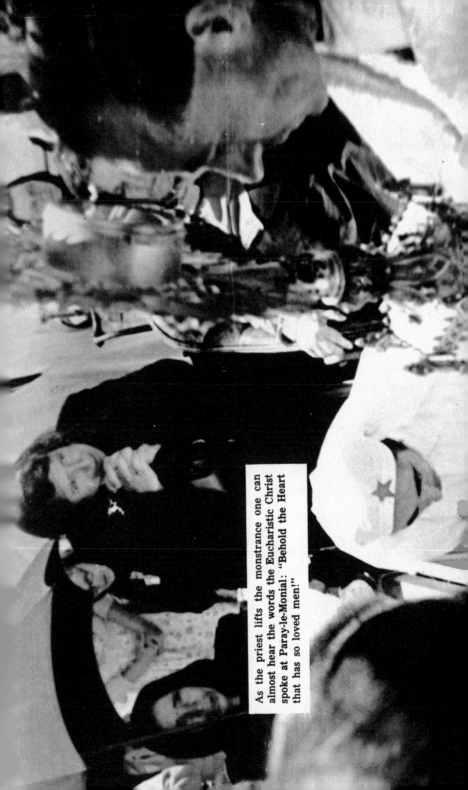

As the priest lifts the monstrance one can almost hear the words the Eucharistic Christ spoke at Paray-le-Monial: "Behold the Heart that has so loved men!"

He asked her to make known through her confessor that He promised to those who would make a Communion of reparation on nine consecutive First Fridays *the grace of a happy death.*

Several million Christians in the world today have made the nine First Fridays.* Often they now also make the First Saturdays* (a similar devotion requested at Fatima), and *many go on to become daily communicants.* Although it is possible that a person can communicate thoughtlessly and without devotion, few people make the effort to communicate often without putting a certain amount of fervor into the act. Certainly it is logical to suppose that God will reward a person of fervor with more than enough grace at the time of death to save his soul. (Whether or not he accepts that grace, as is always the case, is of course up to him. We are free beings; we can either accept or reject God's gifts.) The Promises have provided the incentive many people need to go to Communion more often. As we said earlier, the First Friday devotion is very popular and the First Saturday devotion is growing.

It is lamentable that the Holy Hour devotion is not nearly so popular. Few hear the plaint of Christ still echoing from the Garden of Gethsemane on the night that He instituted the Eucharist, the night He made a stone prison a tabernacle, the night before He died. But His plaint can still touch a sensitive heart: "Could you not watch one hour with Me?"

Has the Christian world forgotten those words He spoke to Peter, James and John as He prayed just a stone's throw from them and saw passing before His eyes the evil of all time, the murders, the deceits, the cruelties, the betrayals, the sacrileges?

Why did He rise from His knees after a time and go to the three who slept? Why did He awaken them to plead for their company? Why did He beg them to resist the lure of sleep?

Above all, why had He chosen the three who most certainly knew He was God, the three whom He had invited to witness Him transfigured on Tabor? And why did He go to them a second time; and a third time? He was the same Christ Who knew that Lazarus was dead and announced that fact to the apostles before they came to Bethany. He was the same Christ Who told the Samaritan woman at the well about her five husbands. Yes, He knew that those chosen ones in Gethsemane would not be able to resist sleep: "The spirit is willing but the flesh is weak."

So what was the reason for accosting them as He did?

Are not we modern believers His reason, we who have lived or will live after that tragic night? In God's eternal present, were His words not meant

to reach us chosen ones who share His Eucharistic
life, the life He had just begun a few hours before
the agony in Gethsemane, but a life which His disciples did not then fully understand?

Today there are some chosen ones who look at
the empty churches where He is neglected and alone,
as on the rock of Gethsemane, and who hear His
plaintive words: "Could you not watch one hour
with Me?"

Some give an hour a day. Still others, following
the saintly Father Mateo, give a prescribed hour a
month from their own homes as they turn their minds
to the nearest tabernacle. Some give an entire night
to the morning of the First Saturday.

How much time will I give Him?[1]

There is one thing *everyone* can and certainly
should do . . . something requiring no more than
thirty seconds a day: *An offering* in the morning
(preferably at the moment of waking) of all our
works of the day *in union with the Eucharistic Sacrifice* taking place in every part of the world.

Pope John XXIII urged this practice on every-

[1] In 1960, the Bishop of Fatima conferred with Pope John XXIII,
who had opened the famous "1960 secret" of Fatima, and then
sent a letter to all Bishops of the world asking for an all-night
vigil of reparation to the Blessed Sacrament on October 12th-
13th of that year. Three hundred dioceses joined around the
world. Pope John sent a cable of blessing and thanks to all
who responded. Subsequently the all-night vigil, promoted
especially by the Blue Army of Our Lady of Fatima in the
U. S., has been made by an increasing number of generous souls.

one. One of the last major things he did before his death was to grant the highest privilege in the Pope's power to those who would offer their sufferings daily, using any words they chose. A short time later he granted the same to those who would offer their works.

Some will be impatient to participate personally in the Liturgy to "eat the bread of life". Some will add some hours of adoration. Some will give an entire night. Some may even become Eucharistic apostles like those mentioned in Chapter XIII.

But all can make a half-minute beginning. (See BLUE ARMY, page 280).

CHAPTER XVI

THE SECRET TODAY

THIS BOOK COULD just as well have been called "The World's Greatest Mystery". But we have preferred to refer to the Eucharist as the World's Greatest Secret because that is what It was when Christ first presented It to the world by the sea of Galilee; this is what It remained during the early centuries of the Church; this is what It is to most persons outside of Christian Communion in the world today.

As was to be expected, Ecumenical Council Vatican II was enormously preoccupied with this Mystery, this Secret of Christian life. Perhaps few effects of the Council have been more palpable. The changes in the Eucharistic arrangements have been so extreme that if a person had been spirited out of this world before the Council and suddenly returned now, he might not know that he was in a Catholic Church when he looked at the sanctuary. He might even have greater doubts as the Mass progressed with the priest facing the congregation, prayers in the vernacular, lectern on the side of the altar, and even a different prayer used at the distribution of Communion.

The most notable change in the church itself

238

would be the location of the tabernacle, which up until the time of the Ecumenical Council was the most prominent feature in every Catholic Church. Indeed it would seem that the altar was designed largely to support the tabernacle, and the ornamentation behind and around the altar used as a decoration or background to the tabernacle.

Now sometimes it might be difficult to know where the tabernacle is located. The altar is moved forward, standing like a table in the center of the sanctuary. It is possible that the small elevation on top of the table would hide a tabernacle hanging beneath it. Yes, in many churches this will be the case. Or might it be that a simple structure covered by a veil, off to one side with no ornamentation around it, might be discerned as the repository of Christ physically present in our midst because of a red light burning closer to this spot than to some other? Yes, in some churches it would be like this.

In other churches the tabernacle still would be central, with an ornate reredos to declare the splendor of its Royal Inhabitant, and another altar used for the sacrifice of the Mass will have been erected some distance in front of it.

The reason for these variations, of course, will be the individual zeal and sense of artistry with which each pastor will have applied the rulings of the Ecumenical Council concerning the Eucharist and the Eucharistic liturgy. But the reason behind all of these changes is simple:

The essence of the Eucharist, as the Council emphasized, is sacrifice. As a wonderful consequence of this sacrifice, the Presence of Christ is in our midst.

As was said earlier in these pages, the Eucharistic liturgy *makes Calvary present*. The moment of consecration gives the participant his own deepest, greatest moment of intimacy with the Divine.

The psalmist said: "What shall I render unto the Lord for all that He has given me?"

While the psalmist could not answer this question in the days of the Old Testament, modern man can answer: "I could give Him back His own Son, nailed to a cross in reparation for my sins and for the sins of the world." And this is the heart of the world's greatest Secret.

In the prayers said during and just after the consecration, we find the full meaning of the Eucharistic liturgy:

Who, the day before He suffered, took bread into His holy and venerable hands, and having raised His eyes to heaven, to You, O God, His Almighty Father, giving thanks to You, He blessed it, broke it, and gave it to His disciples, saying: ALL OF YOU TAKE AND EAT OF THIS: FOR THIS IS MY BODY.

In like manner, when the supper was done, taking also this goodly chalice into His holy and venerable hands, again giving thanks to You, He blessed it, and gave it to His disciples, saying: ALL OF YOU TAKE AND DRINK OF THIS: FOR THIS IS THE CHALICE OF MY BLOOD OF THE NEW AND ETERNAL COVENANT: THE MYSTERY OF FAITH: WHICH SHALL BE SHED FOR YOU AND FOR MANY UNTO THE FORGIVENESS OF SINS. AS OFTEN AS YOU SHALL DO THESE THINGS, IN MEMORY OF ME SHALL YOU DO THEM.

Mindful, therefore, O Lord, not only of the blessed passion of the same Christ, Your Son, our Lord, but also of His resurrection from the dead, and finally His glorious ascension into heaven, we, Your ministers, as also Your holy people, offer to Your supreme Majesty, of the gifts bestowed upon us, the pure Victim, the holy Victim, the all perfect Victim: the holy Bread of life eternal and the Chalice of unending salvation.

And this deign to regard with gracious and kindly attention and hold acceptable, as You deigned to accept the offerings of Abel, Your just servant, and the sacrifice of Abraham our patriarch, and that which Your chief priest Melchisedec offered to You, a holy sacrifice and a spotless victim.

Most humbly we implore You, Almighty God, bid these offerings to be brought by the hands of Your holy angel to Your altar above; before the face of Your divine Majesty; that those of us who, by shar-

ing in the sacrifice of this altar, shall receive the most sacred Body and Blood of Your Son, may be filled with every grace and heavenly blessing. Through the same Christ our Lord. Amen.

One day it is to be expected that most Christian churches once again will have a similar aspect, but for some time to come the tabernacles will be located in various positions, depending on how the pendulum of emphasis on Christ's Presence in our midst has swung in the minds of individual pastors.

There is no doubt that since the Middle Ages the emphasis on Christ's Presence in our midst in the Eucharist has sometimes come to be regarded with even greater reverence than the essential *reason* for His Presence, namely the Act of Sacrifice, the Renewal of Calvary.

Many Christians were even receiving Communion outside of the Eucharistic Sacrifice. Before the Ecumenical Council some steps were taken to curb this, in both the Anglican and Roman Church.

Extremes are usually to be avoided, and it might seem to some that to have the tabernacle made inconspicuous is an extreme. In some churches an excellent solution has been found by giving a reverent location to the tabernacle in the apse of the church or in a special chapel. It might be interesting to note that in the very special Chapel of the Visitation Convent in Paray le Monial the tabernacle has been very ingeniously incorporated into the altar itself, but not receded so completely as to appear of less importance than the altar. In this way it is identified with the table of Sacrifice.

We have chosen to present a picture of this Chapel of Paray le Monial as it was up until the time of the Ecumenical Council and as it is now. Subjectively (since many Christians are going through this period of change with various degrees of subjective emotion) we might say that it was quite a shock to us to come into this Chapel, where Christ appeared out of the Eucharist to make his "final appeal for the love of men", after the altar was changed. We had so often prayed in this Chapel and marveled that it had remained "unchanged" since the day that Christ came forth from the monstrance to Saint Margaret Mary.

But the emotional adjustment is very quickly made with realization of the importance of constantly identifying Christ's Presence in the Eucharist with the Sacrifice which gives us His Presence. There is only one return which Christ wishes from us, and that is sorrow for our sins and prayer for the conversion of sinners. The great lament to the world in the messages of Lourdes and Fatima were: "So many souls are lost because there is no one to pray and to make sacrifices for them." And of what use is it for us to go and feel comfortable in the Presence of Christ in the Eucharist and to miss the opportunity given to us in each Sacrifice of the Mass to bring to bear upon the world the enormous sacrificial force of Calvary?

It is thought possible that *any* Christian could make it possible for a thousand souls to be saved, who otherwise would be damned, by worthily participating in *even one single Sacrifice of the Eucharist*. It is a common belief that if any one of us could identify with the Heart of Mary as she kneels at the foot of the Cross and offers her Divine Son to the Father for the conversion of sinners, we would in that moment become a power like that of Therese of Lisieux, Francis of Assisi, Anthony of Padua.

For many of us the world's greatest Secret will remain a secret. For some, the Secret will yield Its meaning bit by bit, or perhaps even in one great flash of light.

Nevertheless this Secret, this Mystery, will increasingly become the focal point of man on this planet. It may have grown in importance more in the last 500 years, during which Christians for the first time began to question It, than It did in the first 1500 years when there was hardly a doubt.

Today no major city in Christian nations of the world is without a church where the Eucharist is reserved. Often it is the richest, most impressive structure in the entire city.

But there are two major places in the Holy Land that are not commemorated by churches; the place where the Eucharist was instituted and the place of the Ascension. Why?

Why is there nothing but a tiny room about fifteen feet in diameter on the spot where Christ left this earth? Why is there no great church on the spot where He ascended into heaven forty days after His resurrection?

There may be various reasons, but we like to think it is because God did not want to commemorate a spot where Christ seemed to be leaving the world.

The very emptiness of these sacred spots on the Mount of Olives and on Mount Zion recalls the truth that suddenly became clear to the apostles at Pentecost: *He had not really left them at all.* He had been with them in the limited area of Palestine. Now He was to be with all men everywhere, physically, really.

When the early Christians received the Holy Spirit sent to them by Christ as He had promised just before the ascension, they suddenly and wonderfully and clearly understood this. There in that same Cenacle room where He had given them the Eucharist for the first time *the Pentecostal light opened their eyes to the Eucharistic Christ more intimately present than He had ever been before.* They went forth to preach Him, to live for Him, to die for Him, to give Him to us today not in the Cenacle but *in churches in every corner of the world.* Only one of the twelve apostles (excluding Judas) died in Jerusalem. All the others died establishing Christ's Church in different parts of the world. Even the one who was beheaded in Jerusalem had just returned from preaching the Eucharistic Christ in the farthest western limit of the known world.

But what about those of us who doubt?

Can we not, with just a thought, turn to the Mother of Christ, to ask her intercession that we, too, may realize this more fully? Can we not feel the need to tell the Truth-giving Spirit, Love Itself, that our minds are too small, our sins too great, our wills too weak, our habits too gross, our way of thought too careless and shallow to enable us to believe firmly without divine help? Can we not feel the need to pray for our own Pentecost, that His light may pierce the dark pall of our doubts and fears?

We may look up toward that white disc which shines in the monstrance as toward the chink through which, for just a moment, shines the Light of the other world. For St. John writes: "In Him was Life, and the Life was the light of men. The Light shines in the darkness and the darkness did not understand it . . . He was in the world, and the world came to be through Him, and the world did not acknowledge Him . . ."

He is in the world now. That fact cannot be insisted upon too often. But how many of us can really know Him? How many of us really acknowledge Him?

Pilgrims gather at the place of the Ascension where Christ was last seen by the Church gathered together. There is no church here. The rings in the wall are for the tents where liturgy is celebrated on the anniversary of the Ascension.

What about Christians, and even non Christians, who have never actually received Communion? Do they have no "life" in them?

It was the special vocation of Pope John XXIII to emphasize to the world . . . even to apparent atheists . . . that God judges and visits men within the limits and the lights of each. To Pope John, *most* were brothers. Who would not receive Communion if he knew and believed all that has been said of it in this book? Only *such* a man has no life in him.

All others have it as an object of desire, an unacknowledged center of their lives.

The tragedy of Christian disunity is never more evident than in the presence of this Sacrament of Unity. How much of that tragedy lies at the door of those who profess belief in It? And how great a responsibility lies upon those who possess It!

Sometimes we argue: But if He is here, why doesn't He do something to straighten out this mad, evil world? Why doesn't He sweep away slave-labor camps? Why doesn't He end wars, perfidy, conflicts and injustices of all kinds?

The answer is clear: These evils result from neglecting and rejecting Him. That was the message of Fatima, confirmed by a pre-announced public miracle witnessed in our own day by some 100,000 witnesses! He makes Himself peculiarly available and accessible in the Eucharist, but He does not force us to accept Him.

We must reach out to Him if we are to increase the love among men which abolishes these evils and brings peace.

Cardinal Montini of Milan, who later became Paul VI, said in a public speech: "We shall love our neighbors and those far afield. We shall love our country, we shall love other people. We shall love Catholics, the schismatics, the Protestants, the Africans, the indifferent, the Moslems, the pagans and the atheists. We shall love those who merit and those who do not merit being loved."

Where, oh where can we find such love? A love that embraces such a conglomeration of human creatures.

After Cardinal Montini became Pope he told the world where he expected such love to be found. He wrote an encyclical on the Eucharist which we are appending to these pages.

In an earlier chapter we mentioned the Eucharistic vision of the Patriarch of Constantinople, first made public in March, 1967. After describing his vision of the Eucharist the Patriarch said: "I should like to visit the Pope in Rome as soon as possible. The church and the world are surfeited with gestures and nice words. We must go straight to the point. Jesus said to Simon: *Put out into the deep and let down your nets for a catch. And Simon an-*

Eugene Cardinal Tisserant, Dean of the Sacred College of Cardinals, raises the Eucharist in blessing over the sick at Fatima.

*swered, Master, we toiled all night and took nothing!
But at your words I will let down our nets. And when
they had done this, they enclosed a great shoal of fish.*
Think of it, just think of it! With Saint Peter in the
West and Saint John in the East, one vast net could
be thrown in the sea of the world and encircle with
love all those 900 million Christians." (See ATHEN-
AGORAS, page 279)

Ultimately the secret of Christianity is Christ
Himself *as a Living, Present Reality,* a Divine Love
meeting human love.

It will always remain a secret in the sense that
it is the secret of the fidelity of many Christians,
the unrecognized source of their strength in the face
of hardship and trial, and the wellspring of their
holiness.

For others in our modern world it is a secret in
the sense that they do not know about it, or if they
know about it in some sort of cursory way, they ig-
nore it or turn their back upon it. And so they live
in darkness, tragically miserable not realizing that
a remedy is at hand.

Today several small nations which claim to be
Christian, but which are dominated exclusively by
those who no longer believe in the Eucharist, are
the world's unhappiest people. They have the highest suicide rate per capita of all nations on earth
despite extremely high standards of living [1] Cur-

[1] Denmark, Norway and Sweden.

rently they are plunged into an agonized God-searching reminiscent of the Mycenean Age.

All Christians sooner or later must come to the realization that they cannot turn from Christ at Capharnaum, shrug their shoulders and say: "This saying is too hard. Who can accept it?"

Whether they be the leaders of 214 divisions of the church meeting in Geneva, or 2,500 Bishops meeting in Rome, the voice they hear is from the same discourse the night before He died: "This is My Body. This is My Blood . . . Father, I pray that they may be one as You and I are One."

The central reality of Christianity always will be unity with the submission of Christ's human will to His Father. And the Eucharistic Liturgy looms up to such vast importance because it makes the peak of Christ's submission (the sacrifice of Calvary) actually present.

Perhaps a lifetime of prayer and study would not suffice to plumb the depths of the above statement. It certainly is not the purpose of this book to try. But it is enough for the average Christian to know that any person can most easily enter into this sublime identification with the obedience of Christ by daily participation in the Eucharistic Liturgy.

All are obliged to participate once a week. But how much spiritual growth is possible if we limit ourselves to this minimum? And how much if we

Christ is here." were the often repeated words at the 1964 Eucharistic Congress in Bombay. Pope Paul VI came to celebrate the Eucharistic liturgy in this global gathering to honor Christ among us.

fail to prepare ourselves and bring to bear a maximum of attention?

Some cannot participate in the liturgy each day, but all can meditate on the liturgy of the Word and say the prayers, climaxed by spiritual communion, in union with the Eucharistic miracle taking place in every other part of the world ". . . not a new body, for he has only one; but an extension to His body, or better, a transposition of His body into a new dimension."

All that we have tried to say in this book may be summarized in a few paragraphs based on Saint Mark:

The world's greatest secret began on a mountain in Palestine with the miracle of the loaves and the incredible words: "I am Bread from Heaven . . . you must eat My flesh . . ." Pictures of this miracle became the most frequently used by early Christians as modern archeologists have discovered.

We used an entire chapter to describe this event almost at the very beginning. Everyone went away when Christ said that He would give His flesh to eat and His blood to drink, and that they would not live if they did not eat Him. But the apostles themselves, though deeply shaken, did not leave.

Immediately after this Christ sent the apostles across the sea.

A severe storm arose. They were rowing against heavy seas, fearfully straining to gain the shore, when

Pope Paul VI prays in the Cenacle during the Ecumenical Council, recalling those words spoken here by Christ the night He instituted the Eucharist: "Father, that they may be one as you and I are One."

suddenly a ghostly figure moved over the waves. It seemed to pass them. Saint Mark says:

"He would have passed them by. But seeing Him walk upon the sea they thought it was a ghost and cried out for they all saw Him and were afraid. Then immediately He spoke to them: 'Take courage. Do not be afraid. It is I.'"

Why did Christ put them to such a test? Their cries seem to indicate sheer terror. Why did He, who loved them so much, pretend to go by in the storm?

Saint Mark (VI, 45-46) explains:

"They were utterly beside themselves with astonishment for they had not yet understood about the loaves because their hearts were blind."

True, they had not gone away like the others. But like many Christians today, they had not remained because they truly believed they would one day eat His flesh but rather because, as Peter said: "To Whom else could we go?"

After the terror-lesson of the storm, Christ calmed the wind. He proceeded to perform so many miracles that people began to forget the hard saying and again they wanted to proclaim Him King. Saint Mark says: ."*And He got into the boat with them and the wind fell . . . They came to the shore . . . and wherever He went, into village, hamlet or town, they laid the sick in the squares and entreated Him to let them touch but the tassel of His cloak. And as*

many as touched Him were saved." Finally He called
Lazarus from his grave in the presence of a host of
witnesses, and they broke branches from the trees,
laid cloaks in His path, and called Him King even
up to the very gates of the temple.

But it was to fulfill the hard saying that He
had come. This was to be not only the secret of His
church but His greatest gift to men: Bread which
would enable them never to die. So He chose a supper instead of a crown. He chose bread and wine to
perform the first of innumerable transubstantiations
and then immediately performed the miracle of Lazarus in Himself as His final proof.

What a mystery and lesson ring out today in
those incredible words of Saint Mark describing the
frightened disciples in the endangered ship: *"They
were utterly beside themselves . . . because they had
not understood about the loaves."*

Millions of doubting, divided disciples of Christ
have huddled through the storms of two global wars.
Before the now rising waves of the atomic armament
race they seem to know, collectively, that this is a
fateful hour for them. They strain at the oars with
pleas for ecumenism.* Frightened cries rise from a
building in New York where they have been striving
to establish unity under law, only to be thwarted
again and again by waves of atheistic anarchism. The
storm mounts as the ship of the world lists in Asia.

So far the cries of fear do not have the shrill of

sheer terror. And no one claims to have seen a spectre moving over the waves, unless it might be the miracle of the sun at Fatima performed at a specified time and place "So that everyone may believe."

But if we were looking for one, profound explanation of the modern storm, might we not find it in that simple sentence of Saint Mark:

"They had not yet understood the miracle of the loaves because their hearts were blind"?

Could it not be that too many have followed Christ simply because they know He has words of eternal life rather than because they recognize the world's greatest secret, *because they understand the miracle of the loaves?*

He could cure at a distance, but He preferred to be touched and to touch . . . even with as intimate an element as spittle. [1] He preferred to give of Himself by touch . . ., ". . . and as many as touched Him were saved." And He has remained through the mystery of transubstantiated bread *to touch and be touched now.*

Thus the world's greatest secret becomes the world's greatest hope. At this very moment another heart which might have passed by in the storm may be hearing His voice from a nearby tabernacle:

"Do not be afraid. It is I."

---

[1] Mark VIII, 23

EPILOGUE

POPE PAUL AT FATIMA WITH NUN WHO SAW VISIONS

MORE OF WHAT WAS WRITTEN for this book has been omitted than has been included. In particular we omitted the great strides theologians have made in Eucharistic study.

However, for a final and late summary of the position taken by theologians we reproduce here Paul VI's encyclical *The Mystery of Faith*. Additional copies can be obtained for three cents a copy in quantities of fifty or more from Our Sunday Visitor Press, Inc., Huntington, Indiana. To parallel the various arguments in the encyclical with those which have been presented in the previous pages might make an interesting study group project.

The Mystery of Faith

BY HIS HOLINESS, POPE PAUL VI

Paul VI, by Divine Providence pope, to our venerable brothers, the patriarchs, primates, arch-bishops, bishops and other local ordinaries in peace and communion with the Holy See, and to all the clergy and faithful the world: On the doctrine and worship of the Holy Eucharist. Venerable Brothers and Dear Sons: health and Apostolic Benediction.

The Catholic Church has always devoutly guarded as a most precious treasure the mystery of Faith, that is, the ineffable gift of the Eucharist which she received from Christ her spouse as a pledge of His immense love, and during the Second Vatican Council in a new and solemn demonstration she professed her faith and veneration for this mystery. When dealing with the restoration of the sacred Liturgy, the Fathers of the council, by reason of their pastoral concern for the whole Church, considered it of the highest importance to exhort the faithful to participate actively with sound faith and with the utmost devotion in the celebration of this most Holy Mystery, to offer it with the priest to God as a sacrifice for their own salvation and for that of the whole world, and to find in it spiritual nourishment.

For if the sacred liturgy holds the first place in the life of the Church, the Eucharistic Mystery stands at the heart and center of the liturgy, since it is the font of life by which we are cleansed and strengthened to live not for ourselves but for God, and to be united in love among ourselves.

To make evident the indissoluble bond which exists between Faith and devotion, the Fathers of the council, confirming the doctrine which the Church has always held and taught and which was solemnly defined by the Council of Trent, determined to introduce their treatise on the most Holy Mystery of the Eucharist with the following summary of truths:

"At the Last Supper, on the night He was handed over, our Lord instituted the Eucharistic Sacrifice of His Body and Blood, to perpetuate the sacrifice on the Cross throughout the ages until He should come, and thus entrust to the Church, His beloved Spouse, the memorial of His death and resurrection: A sacrament

261

of devotion, a sign of unity, a bond of charity, a paschal banquet in which Christ is received, the soul is filled with Grace and there is given to us the pledge of future glory" (Constit. "De Sacra Liturgia," C. 2. N. Rush A.A.S. LVI, 1964 p. 113).

In these words are highlighted both the sacrifice, which pertains to the essence of the Mass which is celebrated daily, and the sacrament in which the faithful participate in Holy Communion by eating the Flesh of Christ and drinking His Blood, receiving both Grace, the beginning of eternal life, and the medicine of immortality. According to the words of our Lord: "The man who eats my flesh and drinks my blood enjoys eternal life, and I will raise him up at the last day" (John, 6, 55).

Therefore we earnestly hope that the restored sacred liturgy will bring forth abundant fruits of Eucharistic devotion, so that the Holy Church, under this saving sign of piety, may make daily progress toward perfect unity (Cf. John 17-23) and may invite all Christians to a unity of faith and of love, drawing them gently, thanks to the action of Divine Grace.

We seem to have a preview of these fruits and, as it were, to gather in the early results not only in the genuine joy and eagerness with which the members of the Catholic Church have received both the Constitution on the Sacred Liturgy and the restoration of the liturgy, but also in the great number of well-prepared publications which seek to investigate more profoundly and to understand more fruitfully the doctrine on the Holy Eucharist, with special reference to its relation with the mystery of the Church.

All of this is for us a cause of profound consolation and joy. It is a great pleasure for us to communic this to you, Venerable Brothers, that along with us you may g thanks to God, the Giver of all gi Who with His spirit rules the Chu and enriches her with increasing v tues.

REASONS FOR PASTORAL CONCERN AND ANXIETY

However, Venerable Brothers this very matter which we are c cussing, there are not lacking r sons for serious pastoral concern a anxiety. The awareness of our Ap tolic Duty does not allow us to silent in the face of these proble Indeed, we are aware of the fact tl among those who deal with this m Holy Mystery in written or spol word, there are some who, with r erence either to Masses which celebrated in private, or to the d ma of Transubstantiation, or to de tion to the Eucharist, spread abr opinions which disturb the faith and fill their minds with no lit confusion about matters of Faith. is as if everyone were permitted consign to oblivion a doctrine alrea defined by the Church, or else to i terpret it in such a way as to weak the genuine meaning of the words the recognized force of the conce involved.

To confirm what we have said examples, it is not allowable to er phasize what is called the "commu al" Mass to the disparagement Masses celebrated in private, or exaggerate the element of sacrame tal sign as if the symbolism, which a certainly admit in the Eucharist, e presses fully and exhausts complete the mode of Christ's presence in tl sacrament. Nor is it allowable to di cuss the Mystery of Transubstanti tion without mentioning what t

uncil of Trent stated about the
arvelous conversion of the whole
bstance of the bread into the Body
d of the whole substance of the
ne into the Blood of Christ, speak-
g rather only of what is called
"ransignification" and "Transfigur-
ion", or finally to propose and act
on the opinion according to which,
the consecrated Hosts which re-
ain after the celebration of the sac-
fice of the Mass, Christ our Lord
no longer present.

Everyone can see that the spread
these and similar opinions does
eat harm to the Faith and devotion
the Divine Eucharist.

And therefore, so that the hope
oused by the council, that flourish-
g of Eucharistic piety which is now
ervading the whole Church, be not
ustrated by this spread of false
inions, we have with apostolic au-
ority decided to address you, Ven-
able Brothers, and to express our
ind on this subject.

We certainly do not wish to deny
those who are spreading these sin-
lar opinions the praiseworthy ef-
rt to investigate this lofty mystery
d to set forth its inexhaustible
ches, revealing its meaning to the
en of today; rather we acknowl-
dge and approve their effort. How-
ver, we cannot approve the opinions
hich they express, and we have the
ty to warn you about the grave
anger which these opinions involve
r correct faith.

MYSTERY OF FAITH

First of all, we wish to recall
mething which is well known to
ou but which is altogether neces-
ry for repelling every virus of ra-
onalism, something to which many
lustrious martyrs have witnessed
ith their blood, while celebrated

Fathers and Doctors of the Church
constantly professed and taught it;
that is, that the Eucharist is a very
great Mystery. In fact, properly speak
ing, and to use the words of the
Sacred Liturgy, it is the Mystery of
Faith. "Indeed, in it alone," as Leo
XIII, our predecessor of happy memory very wisely remarked, "are contained, in a remarkable richness and
variety of miracles, all supernatural
realities" (Encyclical Mirao Caritatis, Acta Leonis XIII, Vol. XXIII,
1902-1903, p. 122).

We must therefore approach especially this Mystery with humble
respect, not following human arguments, which ought to be silent, but
adhering firmly to Divine Revelation.

St. John Chrysostom, who, as
you know, treated of the Eucharistic
Mystery with such nobility of language and insight born of devotion,
instructing his faithful on one occasion about this Mystery, expressed
these most fitting words:

"Let us submit to God in all
things and not contradict Him, even
if what He says seems contrary to
our reason and intellect; Rather let
His words prevail over our reason
and intellect. Let us act in this way
with regard to the (Eucharistic)
mysteries, looking not only at what
falls under our senses but holding on
to His Words. For His Word cannot
lead us astray" (in Matth. Homil. 82,
4, Migne p. g. 58, 743).

The scholastic Doctors often
made similar affirmations: That in
this Sacrament are the true Body of
Christ and His true Blood is something that "cannot be apprehended
by the senses," says St. Thomas, "but
only by Faith which relies on Divine
Authority. This is why, in a com-

ment on Luke, 22, 19: ('This is my body which is given for you') St. Cyril says: 'Do not doubt whether this is true, but rather receive the Words of the Saviour in Faith, for since He is the Truth, He cannot lie'" (Summ Theol. III Q. 75 A.L.C.).

Thus the Christian people, echoing the words of the same St. Thomas, frequently sing the words: "Sight, touch, and taste in Thee are each deceived, the ear alone most safely is believed. I believe all the Son of God has spoken—than truth's own word there is no truer token."

In fact, St. Bonaventure asserts: "There is no difficulty about Christ's presence in the Eucharist as in a sign, but that He is truly present in the Eucharist as He is in heaven, this is most difficult. Therefore to believe this is especially meritorius" (in IV Sent. Dist. X. P. I Art Un. Qu. I, Oper Omn. Tom. IV Ad Claras Acquas 1889, p. 217).

Moreover, the Holy Gospel alludes to this when it tells of the many disciples of Christ who, after listening to the sermon about eating His Flesh and drinking His Blood, turned away and left our Lord, saying: "This is strange talk, who can be expected to listen to it?" Peter, on the other hand, in reply to Jesus' question whether also the twelve wished to leave, expressed his faith and that of the others promptly and resolutely with the marvelous answer: "Lord, to whom should we go? Thy words are the words of eternal life" (John 6, 61-69).

It is logical, then, that we should follow as a guiding star in our investigations of this Mystery the magisterium of the Church, to whi the Divine Redeemer entrusted protection and for explanation t Revelation which He has commu cated to us through Scripture or Tr dition. For we are convinced th "what since the days of antiqui was preached and believed throug out the whole Church with tr Catholic Faith is true, even if it not submitted to rational investig tion, even if it is not explained means of words" (St. Augustin Contr. Julian VI. 511, Migne. p. 44, 929).

But this is not enough. Havi safeguarded the integrity of t Faith, it is necessary to safeguar also its proper mode of expressio lest by the careless use of words, occasion (God forbid) the rise false opinions regarding faith in th most sublime of mysteries. St. A gustine gives a stern warning abou this in his consideration of the wa of speaking employed by the philos ophers and of that which ought be used by Christians.

"The philosophers," he say "speak freely without fear of offenc ing religious listeners on subjec quite difficult to understand. We, o the other hand, must speak accord ing to a fixed norm, lest the lack restraint in our speech result in som impious opinion even about th things signified by the words them selves" (De Civit. Dei, 23 p. 1. 4 300).

The Church, therefore, with th long labor of centuries and, no without the help of the Holy Spiri has established a rule of languag and confirmed it with the authorit of the councils. This rule, which ha more than once been the watchword and banner of orthodox faith, must be religiously preserved, and let no one presume to change it at his own pleasure or under the pretext of new science. Who would ever tolerate that the dogmatic formulas used by the ecumenical councils for the Mysteries of the Holy Trinity and the Incarnation be judged as no longer appropriate for men of our times and therefore that others be rashly substituted for them? In the same way, it cannot be tolerated that any individual should on his own authority modify the formulas which were used by the Council of Trent to express belief in the Eucharistic Mystery. For these formulas, like the others which the Church uses to propose the dogmas of Faith, express concepts which are not tied to a certain form of human culture, nor to a specific phase of human culture, nor to one or other theological school. No, these formulas present that part of reality which necessary and universal experience permits the human mind to grasp and to manifest with apt and exact terms taken either from common or polished language. For this reason, these formulas are adapted to men of all times and all places.

It must be admitted that these formulas can sometimes be more clearly and accurately explained. In fact, the acheivement of this goal is highly beneficial. But it would be wrong to give to these expressions a meaning other than the original. Thus, the understanding of the faith should be advanced without threat to its unchangeable truth. It is, in fáct, the teaching of the First Vatican Council that "the same signification (of sacred dogmas) is to be forever retained once our Holy Mother the Church has defined it, and under no pretext of deeper penetration may that meaning be weakened (Constit. Dogm. "De Fide Cathol." c. 4.)

THE MYSTERY OF THE EUCHARIST IS VERIFIED IN THE SACRIFICE OF THE MASS

For the inspiration and consolation of all, we wish to review with you, Venerable Brothers, the doctrine which the Catholic Church has always transmitted and unanimously teaches concerning the Mystery of the Eucharist.

We desire to recall at the very outset what may be termed the very essence of the dogma, namely, that by means of the Mystery of the Eucharist, the Sacrifice of the Cross, which was once offered on Calvary, is remarkably re-enacted and constantly recalled, and its saving power exerted for the forgiveness of those sins which we daily commit (Cf. Concil. Trid., "Doctrina de SS. Missae Sacrificio, Ci.).

Just as Moses with the blood of calves has sanctified the Old Testament (Cf. Exodus 24,8), so also Christ our Lord, through the institution of the Mystery of the Eucharist, with His own Blood sanctified the New Testament, Whose mediator He is. For, as the evangelists narrate, at the Last Supper "He took bread, and blessed and broke it, and gave it to them, saying:

"This is my body, given for you; do this for a commemoration of me." And so with the cup, when supper was ended. This cup, He said, "is the New Testament, in my blood which is to be shed for you" (Luke 22, 19-20; Cf. Matt. 26, 26-28; Mark 14, 22-24). And by bidding the apostles to do this in memory of Him, He made clear His Will that the same sacrifice be forever repeated. This intention of Christ was faithfully executed by the primitive Church through her adherence to the teaching of the apostles and through her gatherings summoned to celebrate the Eucharistic Sacrifice. As St. Luke carefully testifies, "these occupied themselves continually with the apostles' teaching, their fellowship in the breaking of bread, and the fixed times of prayer" (Acts 2,41). From this practice, the faithful used to derive such spiritual strength that it was said of them that "there was one heart and soul in all the company of believers" (Acts 4,32).

Moreover, the Apostle Paul, who has faithfully transmitted to us what he had received from the Lord (I Cor. 11, 23 ff.), is clearly speaking of the Eucharistic Sacrifice when he points out that Christians, precisely because they have been made partakers at the Table of the Lord, ought not take part in pagan sacrifices. "Is not this cup we bless," he says, "a participation in Christ's Blood? Is not the bread we break a participation in Christ's Body? . . . to drink the Lord's cup, and yet to drink the cup of evil spirits, to share the Lord's Feast, and to share the feast of evil spirits, is impossible for you" (1 Cor. 10, 15ff). Foreshadowed by Malachias (1,11), this new offering of the New Testament has always been offered by the Church, in accordance with the teaching of our Lord and the apostles, "not only to atone for the sins of these who have died in Christ but have not yet been completely puri-

fied" (Concil, Trid. Doctr. de SS Missae. Sacrif. c. 2.).

Passing over other citations we recall merely the testimony rendered by St. Cyril of Jerusalem, who wrote the following memorable instructions for his neophytes:

"After the spiritual sacrifice, the unbloody act of worship has been completed. Bending over this propitiatory offering we beg God to grant peace to all the churches, to give harmony to the whole world, to bless our rulers, our soldiers, and our companions, to aid the sick and afflicted, and in general to assist all who stand in need; and then we offer the Victim also for our deceased holy ancestors and bishops and for all our dead. As we do this, we are filled with the conviction that this Sacrifice will be of the greatest help to those souls for whom prayers are being offered in the very presence of our Holy and Awesome Victim."

This holy Doctor closes his instruction by citing the parallel of the crown which is woven for the emperor to move him to pardon exiles: "In the same fashion, when we offer our prayers, offer Christ slaughtered for our sins, beseeching our merciful God to take pity both on them and on ourselves" (Catecheses, 23 [Myst. 5], 8-18; p.g. 33, 1115-1118). St. Augustine testifies that this manner of offering also for the deceased "the Sacrifice which ransomed us" was being faithfully observed in the Church at Rome (Cf. Confess., IX 12, 32; p.l. 32, 777; Cf. Ibid. IX, 11, 27; p.l. 32, 775), and at the same time he observes that the Universal Church was following this custom in her conviction that it had been handed down by the earliest Fathers (Cf. Serm. 172, 2; p.l. 38, 936; Cf. de

Cura Geranda pro Mortuis, 12; p.l. 40, 593).

To shed fuller light on the Mystery of the Church, it helps to realize that it is nothing less than the whole Church which, in union with Christ in His role as Priest and Victim, offers the Sacrifice of the Mass and is offered in it. The Fathers of the Church taught this wondrous doctrine (Cf. St. Augustine, de Civit. Dei, X, 6; p.l. 41, 284). A few years ago our predecessor of happy memory, Pius XII, explained it (Cf. Litt. Encycl. Mediator Dei, A.A.S. XXXIX, 1947, p. 552), and only recently the Second Vatican Council enunciated it in its treatise of the people of God as formulated in its Constitution on the Church (Cf. Const. Dogm. de Ecclesia, C.2, N.11; A.A.S. LVII, 1965, p. 15).

To be sure, the distinction between universal priesthood and hierarchical priesthood is one of essence and not merely one of degree (Cf. Ibid. C.2, N.10; A.A.S. LVII, 1965, p.14), and this distinction should be faithfully observed. Yet we cannot fail to be filled with the earnest desire that this teaching on the Mass be explained over and over until it takes root deep in the hearts of the faithful. Our desire is founded on our conviction that the correct understanding of the Eucharistic Mystery is the most effective means to foster devotion to this sacrament, to extol the dignity of all the faithful, and to spur their spirit toward the attainment of the summit of sanctity, which is nothing less than the total offering of oneself to service of the Divine Majesty.

We should also mention "the public and social nature of every Mass" (Const. de Sacra Liturgia, C.1, N.27; A.A.S. LVI, 1964, p. 107), a conclusion which clearly follows from the doctrine we have been discussing. For even though a priest should offer Mass in private, that Mass is not something private; It is an act of Christ and of the Church. In offering this Sacrifice, the Church learns to offer herself as a sacrifice for all. Moreover, for the salvation of the entire world she applies the single, boundless, redemptive power of the Sacrifice of the Cross. For every Mass is offered not for the salvation of ourselves alone, but also for that of the whole world. Hence, athough the very nature of the action renders most appropriate the active participation of many of the faithful in the celebration of the Mass, nevertheless, that Mass is to be fully approved which, in conformity with the prescriptions and lawful traditions of the Church, a priest for a sufficient reason offers in private, that is, in the presence of no one except his server. From such a Mass an abundant treasure of special salutary graces enriches the celebrant, the faithful, the whole Church, and the entire world — graces which are not imparted in the same abundance by the mere reception of Holy Communion.

Therefore, from a paternal and solicitous heart, we recommend to priests, who bestow on us a special crown of happiness in the Lord, that they be mindful of their power, received through the hands of the ordaining bishop, of offering Sacrifice to God and of celebrating Masses both for the living and for the dead in the name of the Lord (Cf. Pontificabile Romanum), and that they worthily and devoutly offer Mass each day in order that both they and the rest of the faithful may enjoy the benefits that flow so richly from the Sacrifice of the Cross. Thus also they will contribute most to the salvation of the human race.

IN THE SACRIFICE OF THE MASS CHRIST IS MADE SACRAMENTALLY PRESENT

By the few ideas which we have mentioned regarding the Sacrifice of the Mass, we are encouraged to explain a few notions concerning the Sacrament of the Eucharist, seeing that both Sacrifice and Sacrament pertain inseparably to the same Mystery. In an unbloody representation of the Sacrifice of the Cross and in application of its saving power, in the Sacrifice of the Mass the Lord is immolated when, through the words of consecration, He begins to be present in a sacramental form under the appearances of bread and wine to become the spiritual food of the faithful.

All of us realize that there is more than one way in which Christ is present in His Church. We wish to review at greater length the consoling doctrine which was briefly set forth in the constitution "De Sacra Liturgia" (Cf. C. 1, N.7; A.A.S. LVI, 1964, pp. 100-101). Christ is present in His Church when she prays, since it is He who "prays for us and prays in us and to Whom we pray as to our God" (St. Augustine, "in Ps." 85, 1; p.l. 37, 1081). It is He who has promised: "where two or three are gathered together in my name, I am there in the midst of them" (Matt. 18,20). He is present in the Church as she performs her works of mercy, not only because we do to Christ whatever good we do to one of His least brethren (Cf. Matt. 25,40), but also because it is Christ, performing these works through the Church, who

continually assists men with His Divine Love. He is present in the Church on her pilgrimage of struggle to reach the harbor of eternal life, since it is He who through Faith dwells in our hearts (Cf. Eph. 3,17) and, through the Holy Spirit whom He gives us, pours His love into those hearts (Cf. Rom. 5,5).

In still another genuine way He is present in the Church as she preaches, since the Gospel which she proclaims is the Word of God, which is not preached except in the name of Christ, by the authority of Christ and with the assistance of Christ the Incarnate Word of God. In this way there is formed "one flock which trusts its only Shepherd" (Idem, "Contr. Litt. Petiliani" III, 10, 11, p.l. Re, 353).

He is present in His Church as she governs the people of God, since her sacred power comes from Christ, and since Christ, "the Shepherd of Shepherds" (St. Augustine, "in Ps." 86,3; p.l. 37, 1102), is present in the pastors who exercise that power, according to His promise to the apostles: "Behold I am with you all through the days that are coming, until the consummation of the world."

Moreover, in a manner still more sublime, Christ is present in His Church as she offers in His Name the Sacrifice of the Mass; He is present in her as she administers the Sacraments. We find deep consolation in recalling the accurate and eloquent words with which St. John Chrysostom, overcome with a sense of awe, described the presence of Christ in the offering of the Sacrifice of the Mass: "I wish to add something that is plainly awe-inspiring, but do not be astonished or upset. This Sacriice, no matter who offers it, be it Peter or Paul, is always the same as that which Christ gave His disciples and which priests now offer: The offering of today is in no way inferior to that which Christ offered, because it is not men who sanctify the offering of today; it is the same Christ who sanctified His own. For just as the words which God spoke are the very same as those which the priest now speaks, so too the oblation is the very same" ("In Epist. 2 ad Timoth. Homil." 2, p.g. 4; 612). No one is unaware that the Sacraments are the actions of Christ, Who administers them through men. Therefore, the Sacraments are holy in themselves, and by the power of Christ they pour Grace into the soul when they touch the body. The mind boggles at these different ways in which Christ is present; They confront the Church with a mystery ever to be pondered.

But there is yet another manner in which Christ is present in His Church, a manner which surpasses all the others; it is His presence in the Sacrament of the Eucharist, which is for this reason "a more consoling source of devotion, a more lovely object of contemplation, a more effective means of sanctification than all the other sacraments" (Aegidiius Tomanus, "Theoremata de Corpore Christi," Theor. 50, Venetiis 1521, p. 127). The reason is clear; it contains Christ Himself and it is "a kind of perfection of the spiritual life; in a way, it is the goal of all the sacraments" (St. Thomas, Summ. Theol. III, q. 73, a. 3 c.).

This presence is called "real"— by which it is not intended to exclude all other types of presence as if they could not be "real" too, but because it is presence in the fullest sense: that is to say, it is a substantial presence by which Christ, the God-man, is wholly and entirely present (Cf. Conc. of Trent, Decree on the Eucharist, Ch. 3). It would therefore be wrong to explain this presence by having recourse to the "spiritual" nature, as it is called, of the glorified body of Christ, which is present everywhere, or by reducing it to a kind of symbolism, as if this most august Sacrament consisted of nothing else than an efficacious sign "of the spiritual presence of of Christ and of His intimate union with the faithful, members of His Mystical Body" (Pius XII, Encycl. Humani Generis A.A.S. XLII, 1950, p. 578).

It is true that much can be found in the Fathers and in the scholastics with regard to symbolism in the Eucharist, especially with reference to the unity of the Church. The Council of Trent, restating their doctrine, taught that the Savior bequeathed the Blessed Eucharist to His Church "as a symbol . . . of that unity and charity with which He wished all Christians to be most intimately united among themselves," and hence "as a symbol of that one body of which He is the Head" (Decree "On the Eucharist," Proem, and Ch. 2).

When Christian literature was still in its infancy, the unknown author of that work we know as the "Didache or Teaching of the Twelve Apostles" wrote as follows on this subject: "In regard to the Eucharist, give thanks in this manner: . . . Just as this bread was scattered and dispersed over the hills, but when harvested was made one, so may Your Church be gathered into Your Kingdom from the ends of the earth" ("Didache", 9:1 Funk, "Patres Apostolici", 1,20).

The same we read in St. Cyprian, writing in defense of the Church against schism: "Finally, the sacrifices of the Lord proclaim the unity of Christians, bound together by the bond of a firm and inviolable charity. For when the Lord, in speaking of bread which is produced by the compacting of many grains of wheat, refers to it as His Body, He is describing our people whose unity He has sustained, and when He refers to wine pressed from many grapes and berries, as His Blood, He is speaking of our flock, formed by the fusing of many united together" ("Ep. ad Magnum," 7 p.l. en 1189).

But before all of these, St. Paul had written to the Corinthians: the One Bread makes us One Body, though we are many in number the same Bread is shared by all. (I Cor. 10,17).

While the Eucharistic symbolism brings us to an understanding of the effect proper to this Sacrament, which is the unity of the Mystical Body, it does not indicate or explain what it is that makes this Sacrament different from all others. The constant teaching which the Catholic Church passes on to her catechumens, the understanding of the Christian people, the doctrine defined by the Council of Trent, the very words used by Christ when He instituted the Most Holy Eucharist, compel us to acknowledge that "the Eucharist is that flesh of our Savior Jesus Christ who suffered for our sins and whom the Father in his loving-kindness raised again" (St. Ignatius, "Ep. ad Smyrn." Un Qh p.g. 5, 714). To these words of St. Igna-

tius of Antioch, we may add those which Theodore of Mopsueta, a faithful witness to the faith of the Church on this point, addressed to the faithful: "The Lord did not say: This is a symbol of My Body, and this is a symbol of My Blood but: This is My Body and My Blood." He teaches us not to look to the nature of those things which lie before us and are perceived by the senses, for by the prayer of thanksgiving and the words spoken over them, they have been changed into flesh and blood" ("In Math. Comm.," Ch. 26 P.G. 66, 714).

The Council of Trent, basing itself on this faith of the Church, "openly and sincerely professes that within the Holy Sacrament of the Eucharist, after the Consecration of the Bread and Wine, Our Lord Jesus Christ, true God and true Man, is really, truly and substantially contained under those outward appearances." In this way, the Savior in His humanity is present not only at the right hand of the Father according to the natural manner of existence, but also in the Sacrament of the Eucharist "by a mode of existence which we cannot express in words, but which, with a mind illumined by Faith, we can conceive, and must most firmly believe, to be possible to God" (Decree "On the Eucharist," Ch. 1).

CHRIST OUR LORD IS PRESENT IN THE SACRAMENT OF THE EUCHARIST BY TRANSUBSTANTIATION

To avoid misunderstanding, this sacramental presence which surpasses the laws of nature and constitutes the greatest miracle of its kind (Cf. Encycl. "Mirae Caritatis," "Acta Leonis XIII," Vol. XXII, 1902-

1903, p. 123), we must listen with docility to the voice of the teaching and praying Church. This voice, which constantly echoes the voice of Christ, assures us that the way Christ is made present in this Sacrament is none other than by the change of the whole substance of the bread into His Body, and of the whole substance of the wine into His Blood, and that this unique and truly wonderful change the Catholic Church rightly calls Transubstantiation (Cf. Council of Trent, "Decree on the Eucharist," Ch. 4, and Can. 2). As a result of Transubstantiation, the species of bread and wine undoubtedly take on a new meaning and a new finality, for they no longer remain ordinary bread and ordinary wine, but become the sign of something sacred, the sign of a spiritual food. However, the reason they take on this new significance and this new finality is simply because they contain a new "reality" which we may justly term Ontological. Not that there lies under those species what was already there before, but something quite different; and that not only because of the Faith of the Church, but in objective reality, since after the change of the substance or nature of the bread and wine into the Body and Blood of Christ, nothing remains of the bread and wine but the appearances, under which Christ, whole and entire, in His physical "reality" is bodily present, although not in the same way that bodies are present in a given place.

For this reason the Fathers took special care to warn the faithful that in reflecting on this most august Sacrament, they should not trust to their senses, which reach only the properties of bread and wine, but rather to the Words of Christ which have power to transform, change and transmute the bread and wine into His Body and Blood. For, as those same Fathers often said, the power that accomplishes this is that same power by which God Almighty, at the beginning of time, created the world out of nothing.

"We have been instructed in these matters and filled with an unshakeable faith," says St. Cyril of Alexandria, at the end of a sermon on the Mysteries of the Faith, "that that which seems to be bread, is not bread, though it tastes like it, but the Body of Christ, and that which seems to be wine, is not wine, though it too tastes as such, but the Blood of Christ . . . draw inner strength by receiving this bread as spiritual food and your soul will rejoice" ("Catecheses," 22, A9; "Myst." 4). p.g. 33, 1103).

St. John Chrysostom emphasizes this point, saying: "It is not the power of man which makes what is put before us the Body and Blood of Christ, but the power of Christ Himself Who was crucified for us. The priest standing there in the place of Christ says these words but their power and grace are from God. 'This is my body,' he says, and these words transform what lies before him." ("De Prodit. Iudae. Homil." 1, 6, p.g. 49, 380 Cf. "In Matth." "Homil." 82, 5: p.g. 58, 744).

Cyril, Bishop of Alexandria, is in full agreement with the bishop of Constantinople when he writes in his commentary on the Gospel of St. Matthew: "Christ said indicating (the bread and wine): 'This is My Body,' and 'this is My Blood,' in order that you might not judge what you see to be a mere figure. The offerings, by the hidden power of God Almighty, are changed into Christ's Body and Blood, and by receiving these we come to share in the life-giving and sanctifying efficacy of Christ" ("In Matth." 26, 27; p.g. 72, 451).

Ambrose, Bishop of Milan, dealing with the Eucharistic change, says: "Let us be assured that this is not what nature formed, but what the blessing consecrated, and that greater efficacy resides in the blessings than in nature, for by the blessing nature is changed." To confirm the truth of this Mystery, he recounts many of the miracles described in the Scriptures, including Christ's birth of the Virgin Mary, and then turning to the work of Creation, concludes thus: "Surely the word of Christ, which could make out of nothing that which did not exist, can change things already in existence into what they were not. For it is no less extraordinary to give things new natures than to change their natures" ("De Myster.," 9, 50-52; p.l. 16, 422-424).

However, there is no need to assemble many testimonies. Rather let us recall that firmness of faith with which the Church with one accord opposed Berengarius, who, yielding to the difficulties of human reasoning, was the first who dared deny the Eucharistic change. More than once she threatened to condemn him unless he retracted. Thus it was that our predecessor, St. Gregory VII, ordered him to pronounce the following oath: "I believe in my heart and openly profess that the bread and wine which are placed upon the altar are, by the Mystery of the Sacred Prayer and the

Words of the Redeemer, substantially changed into the true and life giving Flesh and Blood of Jesus Christ Our Lord, and that after the Consecration, there is present the true Body of Christ which was born of the Virgin and, offered up for the salvation of the world, hung on the cross and now sits at the right hand of the Father and that there is present the True Blood of Christ which flowed from His side. They are present not only by means of a sign and of the efficacy of the Sacrament, but also in the very reality and truth of their nature and substance" (Mansi "Coll. Ampliss. Concil." XX, 524 d).

These words fully accord with the doctrine of the Mystery of the Eucharistic Change as set forth by the ecumenical councils. The constant teaching of these councils — of the Lateran, of Constance, Florence and Trent—whether stating the teaching of the Church or condemning errors, affords us an admirable example of the unchangingness of the Catholic Faith.

After the Council of Trent, our predecessor, Pius VI, on the occasion of the errors of the Synod of Pistoia, warned parish priests when carrying out their office of teaching, not to neglect to speak of Transubstantiation, one of the articles of the Faith (Const. "Auctorem Fidei," 28 August, 1794). Similarly our predecessor of happy memory, Pius XII, recalled the bounds which those who undertake to discuss the Mystery of Transubstantiation might not cross (Allocutio Habita Die 22 Septembris 1956, 'A.A.S.' CLVII, 1956, p. 720). We ourselves also, in fulfillment of our Apostolic Office, have openly borne solemn witness to the Faith of the Church at the National Eucharistic Congress held recently at Pisa (A.A.S. LVII, 1965, pp. 588-592).

Moreover the Catholic Church has held on to this faith in the presence in the Eucharist of the Body and Blood of Christ, not only in her teaching but also in her practice, since she has at all times given to this great Sacrament the worship which is known as Latria and which may be given to God alone. As St. Augustine says: "It was in His Flesh that Christ walked among us and it is His Flesh that He has given us to eat for our salvation. No one, however, eats of this Flesh without having first adored it . . . and not only do we not sin in thus adoring it, but we would sin if we did not do so" ("In Ps." 98, 9; p.l. 37, 1264).

LATREUTIC WORSHIP OF THE SACRAMENT OF THE EUCHARIST

The Catholic Church has always offered and still offers the cult of Latria to the Sacrament of the Eucharist, not only during Mass, but also outside of it, reserving consecrated Hosts with the utmost care, exposing them to solemn veneration, and carrying them processionally to the joy of great crowds of the faithful.

In the ancient documents of the Church we have many testimonies of this veneration. The pastors of the Church in fact solicitously exhorted the faithful to take the greatest care in keeping the Eucharist which they took to their homes. "The body of Christ is meant to be eaten, not to be treated with irreverence," St. Hipolytus warns the faithful ("Tradit. Apost". Ed Botte, "La Tradition Apostolique de St. Hippolyte", Munster 1963, p.84).

In fact the faithful thought themselves guilty, and rightly so, as Origen recalls, if after they received the body of the Lord in order to preserve it with all care and reverence, a small fragment of it fell off through negligence ("In Exod. Fragm." p.g.12, 391).

The same pastors severely reproved those who showed lack of reverence if it happened. This is attested to by Novitianus whose testimony in the matter is trustworthy. He judged as deserving condemnation anyone who came out of Sunday service carrying with him as usual the Eucharist, the Sacred Body of the Lord, "not going to his house but running to places of amusement" ("De Spectaculis" C.S.E.L. III, p.8).

On the other hand St. Cyril of Alexandria rejects as folly the opinion of those who maintained that if a part of the Eucharist was left over for the following day it did not confer sanctification. "For," he says, neither Christ is altered nor His Holy Body changed, but the force and power and vivifying grace always remain with it" ("Epist. ad Calosyrium" p.g. 76, 1075).

Nor should we forget that in ancient times the faithful, harassed by the violence of persecution or living in solitude out of love for monastic life, nourished themselves even daily, receiving Holy Communion by their own hands when the priest or deacon was absent (Cf. Basil. "Epist." 93, p.g. 32, 483-486).

We say this not in order that there may be some change in the way of keeping the Eucharist and of receiving Holy Communion which was later on prescribed by Church laws and which now remain in force, but rather that we may rejoice over

EPILOGUE

the Faith of the Church which is always one and the same.

This faith also gave rise to the Feast of Corpus Christi which was first celebrated in the Diocese of Liege specially through the efforts of the servant of God, Blessed Juliana of Mount Cornelius, and which our predecessor Urban IV extended to the Universal Church. From it have originated many practices of Eucharistic piety which under the inspiration of Divine Grace have increased from day to day and with which the Catholic Church is striving ever more to do homage to Christ, to thank Him for so great a gift and to implore His mercy.

EXHORTATION TO PROMOTE THE CULT OF THE EUCHARIST

We therefore ask you, Venerable Brothers, among the people entrusted to your care and vigilance, to preserve this Faith in its purity and integrity—a Faith which seeks only to remain perfectly loyal to the Word of Christ and of the apostles and unambiguously rejects all erroneous and mischievous opinions. Tirelessly promote the Cult of the Eucharist, the focus where all other forms of piety must ultimately emerge.

May the faithful, thanks to your efforts, come to realize and experience ever more perfectly the truth of these words: "He who desires life finds here a place to live in and the means to live by. Let him approach, let him believe, let him be incorporated so that he may receive life. Let him not refuse union with the members, let him not be a corrupt member, deserving to be cut off, nor a disfigured member to be ashamed of. Let him be a grateful, fitting and healthy member. Let him cleave to the body, let him live by God and for God. Let him now labor here on earth, that he may afterwards reign in heaven" (St. Augustine "In Ioann. Tract." 26, 13 p.l. 35, 1613).

It is to be desired that the faithful, every day and in great numbers, actively participate in the Sacrifice of the Mass, receive Holy Communion with a pure heart, and give thanks to Christ Our Lord for so great a gift. Let them remember these words: "The desire of Jesus Christ and of the Church that all the faithful receive daily Communion means above all that through the sacramental union with God they may obtain the strength necessary for mastering their passions, for purifying themselves of their daily venial faults and for avoiding the grave sins to which human frailty is exposed" (Decr. S. Congr. Concil., 20 Dec. 1905, Approb. A. S. Pio X, A.A.S. XXXVIII, 1905, p. 501).

In the course of the day the faithful should not omit to visit the Blessed Sacrament, which according to the liturgical laws must be kept in the churches with great reverence in a most honorable location. Such visits are a proof of gratitude, an expression of love, an acknowledgement of the Lord's Presence.

No one can fail to understand that the Divine Eucharist bestows upon the Christian people an incomparable dignity. Not only while the Sacrifice is offered and the Sacrament is received, but as long as the Eucharist is kept in our churches and oratories, Christ is truly the Emmanuel, that is, "God with us." Day and night He is in our midst, He dwells with us, full of Grace and Truth (Cf. John 1,14). He restores morality, nourishes virtues, consoles the afflicted, strengthens the weak. He proposes His own example to those who come to Him that all may learn to be, like Himself, meek and humble of heart and to seek not their own interests but those of God.

Anyone who approaches this august Sacrament with special devotion and endeavors to return generous love for Christ's own infinite love, will experience and fully understand—not without spiritual joy and fruit—how precious is the life hidden with Christ in God (Cf. Col. 3,3) and how great is the value of converse with Christ, for there is nothing more consoling on earth, nothing more efficacious for advancing along the road of holiness.

Further, you realize, Venerable Brothers, that the Eucharist is reserved in the churches and oratories as in the spiritual center of a religious community or of a parish, yes, of the Universal Church and of all humanity, since beneath the appearance of the species, Christ is contained, the Invisible Head of the Church, the Redeemer of the world, the Center of all hearts, "by Whom all things are and by Whom we exist" (I Cor. 8, 6).

From this it follows that the worship paid to the Divine Eucharist strongly impels the soul to cultivate a "social" love (Cf. St. Augustine. De Gen Ad Litt. XI, 15, 20; p.l. 34, 437), by which the common good is given preference over the good of the individual. Let us consider as our own interests of the community, of the parish, of the entire Church, extending our charity to the whole world, because we know that everywhere there are members of Christ.

The Eucharistic Sacrament, Venerable Brothers, is the sign and the cause of the unity of the Mystical Body, and it inspires an active "ecclesial" spirit in those who venerate it with greater fervor. Therefore, never cease to persuade those committed to your care that they should learn to make their own the cause of the Church, in approaching the Eucharistic mystery to pray to God without interruption to offer themselves to God as a pleasing sacrifice for the peace and unity of the Church, so that all the children of the Church be united and think the same, that there be no divisions among them, but rather unity of mind and purpose, as the apostle insists (Cf. 1 Cor. 1, 10). May all those not yet in perfect communion with the Catholic Church, who though separated from her glory in the name of Christian, share with us as soon as possible with the help of Divine Grace that unity of Faith and Communion which Christ wanted to be the distinctive mark of His disciples.

This zeal in praying and consecrating one's self to God for the unity of the Church should be practiced particularly by Religious, both men and women, inasmuch as they are in a special way devoted to the adoration of the Blessed Sacrament, according it homage and honor on earth, in virtue of their vows.

Nothing has ever been or is more important to the Church or more consoling than the desire for the unity of all Christians, a desire which we wish to express once again in the very words used by the Council of Trent at the close of its Decree on the Most Blessed Eucharist: "In conclusion, the sacred synod with paternal love admonishes, exhorts, prays and implores 'through the merciful kindness of our God' (Luke 1, 78) that each and every Christian come at last to a perfect agreement regarding this sign of unity, this bond of charity, this symbol of concord, and, mindful of such great dignity and such exquisite love of Christ our Lord who gave His Beloved Son as the price of our salvation and 'His Flesh to eat' (John 6, 48 ss.) Believe and adore those sacred mysteries of His Body and Blood with such firm and unwavering faith, with such devotion, piety and veneration, that they can receive frequently that super-substantial Bread (Matt. 6. 11), which will be for them truly the life of the soul and unfailing strength of mind, so that fortified by its vigor (Cf. Kings, 19, 1) they can depart from this wretched pilgrimage on earth to reach their heavenly home where they will then eat the same 'Bread of Angels' (Ps. 77, 25) no longer hidden by the species which now they eat under the sacred appearances' (Decr. De SS. Eucharistia, c. 8).

May the all-good Redeemer who shortly before His death prayed to the Father that all who were to believe in Him would be one even as He and the Father were One (Cf. John 17, 20-21), deign speedily to hear our most ardent prayer and that of the entire Church, that we may all with one voice and one Faith, celebrate the Eucharistic Mystery and, by participating in the Body of Christ, become One Body (Cf. I Cor. 10, 17), linked by those same bonds which He Himself desired for its perfection.

And we turn with paternal affection also to those who belong to the Venerable Churches of the Orient, from which came so many most illustrious Fathers whose testimony

to the belief of the Eucharist we have so gladly cited in our present letter. Our soul is filled with intense joy as we consider your Faith in the Eucharist, which is also our Faith, and as we listen to the liturgical prayers by which you celebrate so great a Mystery, we rejoice to behold your Eucharistic devotion, and to read your theologians explaining or defending the doctrine of this most august Sacrament.

May the Most Blessed Virgin Mary from whom Christ Our Lord took the flesh which under the species of bread and wine "is contained, offered and consumed" (C.I.C., Can. 801), may all the saints of God, specially those who burned with a more ardent devotion to the Divine Eucharist, intercede before the Father of Mercies so that from this same faith in and devotion toward the Eucharist may result and flourish a perfect unity of communion among all Christians.

Unforgettable are the words of the holy martyr Ignatius, in his warning to the faithful of Philadelphia against the evils of division and schism, the remedy for which lies in the Eucharist: "Strive then," he says, "to make use of one form of thanksgiving for the Flesh of Our Lord Jesus Christ is one and one in the chalice in the union of His Blood one altar, one bishop" (Epist. Ad Philadelph., 4 p.g. 5, 700).

Given at Rome, at St. Peter's, the third day of September, the Feast of Pope St. Pius X, in the year 1965, the third year of our pontificate.   —— Paul VI, Pope.

WORDS and REFERENCES

(marked in the text with an asterisk)

ACCIDENT: We use the word here in its philosophical meaning of *that which qualifies* a substance, such as color, size, shape, texture, or any quality or property of a thing *which is not essential to it*. (See SUBSTANCE).

ACROSTIC: A composition in which the first or last letter, taken in order, forms a word or phrase. If the acrostic is a word, as Christians used the Greek word for fish, each letter stands for another word.

AGAPE: This is actually a Greek word which we use because it cannot be translated. The closest single synonym in English would be *love*. But agape means divine love in all its dimensions. It means the love God has for us and the love we must have for Him, and for all our fellow men in Him. This love is expressed in the Eucharist, and hence the term is applied to the Eucharistic liturgy, the "Lord's Supper."

ALACOQUE, SAINT MARGARET MARY: No one is bound to believe in the revelations made by this saint (see Chapter XV) because we have only the word of the saint and confirmation of experience. But it is impractical, even irrational, to question them. There is evidence that the saint told the truth, and none that she lied. Papal encyclicals and bulls which affirm belief in these apparitions include PIUS IX: *Brief of Beatification of Margaret Mary*, Sept. 18th, 1864; LEO XII: encyclical *Annum Sacrum*, May

25th, 1899; BENEDICT XV: *Bull of Margaret Mary's canonization*, May 13, 1920; PIUS XI: Encyclical *Miserentissimus*, May 8th, 1928. But above all we see the benefits from the devotion, its universality, its fruits of holiness. Moreover, aside from the promises which Our Lord made when He appeared to Saint Margaret Mary' out of the Eucharist, there is truly nothing new in the devotion but merely an appeal for reparation and love to Christ Who so loves us. Under obedience, Saint Margaret described the revelations in her own words published as "Life and Words." An edition with commentary by Msgr. Gauthey in three volumes was published in Paris in 1920: *Vie et Oeuvres de St. M.-M.* Several miracles have been wrought through the saint's intercession as was proved when she was canonized (see this word).

ANGEL: The figure which appeared to the children of Fatima was radiant, and had appeared before. He identified himself as an angel. We do not concern ourselves with *how* the apparition took place. We have many scriptural precedents of angelic visitations: to Abraham, to Elias, to the Virgin Mary. But for the "initiated" there are perhaps two other questions which arise: Where did the angel obtain the Host? And how can Divinity be offered to Divinity (this latter question seems stupid, but a rather outstanding theologian brought it up). Rev. Messias Coelho, one of the world's greatest students of the subject, presumes that the Host was from some tabernacle. As for the second question: The angel does not offer just the Divinity of Christ to the Divinity of the Holy Trinity (which would indeed be offering Himself to Himself), but offers also Christ's Body, Blood and Soul. And this prayer which the angel taught to the children at Fatima, and which they found afterwards to have been engraved in their memories so that each child remembered it word for word independently of the others, teaches us to offer Christ in the Eucharist to the Blessed Trinity (in adoration, reparation, and petition) *even outside the Eucharistic Liturgy,* and thereby to a degree *extending the Eucharistic Liturgy throughout the day.* The entire prayer taught by the angel is as follows:

"O Most Holy Trinity, Father, Son and Holy Spirit, I bow down before Thee, I adore Thee. I offer Thee the most precious Body, Blood, Soul and Divinity of Jesus Christ, present in all the tabernacles of the world, in reparation for the outrages, sacrileges, and indifference by which He is offended. By the infinite merits of the Sacred Heart of Jesus and the Immaculate Heart of Mary (see this word), I beg the conversion of poor sinners."

ARCHEOLOGISTS: Students of antiquities, such as ancient relics, remains of buildings, old parchments or manuscripts, inscriptions, and the like. Historians deal primarily with facts and events, but archeologists are preoccupied by the things which bear witness to facts and events of ancient times.

ARCHEOLOGY: The science of antiquities. Once it was largely a guessing science, but in modern times it has become more precise due to comparative studies among experts in the field, carbon tests, spectrum analysis, and other modern aids. History usually gives archeology the clues for its discoveries.

ATHENAGORAS I: Patriarch of Constantinople (now called Istanbul), 262nd successor of Saint Andrew and the spiritual leader of over 160 million members of the Orthodox (see this word) Church. He can be likened to Pope John XXIII, whom he knew intimately, and he is perhaps as revered in the Eastern Church as John is in the West. He spent eighteen years in the U. S. as Archbishop of the Orthodox in North and South America. The vision of the "Chalice of Our Lord" which the Patriarch made public in an interview with LIFE reporter Peter Dragadze in March, 1967, is a vision of the Eucharist. The

Orthodox do not communicate with a Host, as in the Latin church. They consecrate bread, then drop the Eucharist into a chalice, and communion is given with a little spoon from the chalice. Many other Christians communicate in the same manner, receiving Christ simultaneously under both species.

BENEDICTION: This is a paraliturgical Eucharistic service which began in the time of the Black Plague, when the Blessed Sacrament was exposed for public adoration. Soon it became a custom before returning the Blessed Sacrament to "hiding" in the tabernacle (see this word) to lift It in benediction upon the adorers. It is permitted on Sundays, Feast Days, during Forty Hours and after all night vigils and on other special occasions. A Monstrance (see this word) is usually used, but not necessarily.

BLUE ARMY of OUR LADY of FATIMA: Founded in 1947 by an American priest (Msgr. Harold V. Colgan) as a response to the conditions given at Fatima for the conversion of Russia and world peace. It was ultimately adopted by the Bishops of Portugal as the official Apostolate of Fatima. Its international center, next to the Basilica at Fatima, was dedicated by Pope Pius XII in 1956 through a Legate, Eugene Cardinal Tisserant, Dean of the College of Cardinals. The first phase of the Blue Army's goal, the conversion of Russia, was considered achieved by the action of Pope Paul VI on the last day of the third session of Vatican Council II (see VATICAN II). The "Army" is a lay movement, uniquely spiritual, with no dues or meetings required except among promoters. Each member is required to say a morning offering and to renew this offering (at least by a thought or intention) in moments of temptation. As aids to remembering the offering, and for spiritual strength and assistance, the members are also required to say the Rosary and wear the brown Scapular (for the importance of these sacramentals in reference to the Eucharist, see reference to Saint Thomas

Aquinas on page 149). These requirements fulfill the basic conditions of the message of Fatima and by 1967 had been promised by over twenty million Blue Army members. It remains a lay movement with diocesan supervision in most instances. Philadelphia's Cardinal O'Hara had said: "It is something which must come from the people." Its most evident fruit is the spirituality of its members from whom grew the international movement of the all-night-vigils (see author's book NIGHT of LOVE, published by AMI, 1967, 176 pp). Cardinal Van Rooey of Belgium said: "It is the most completely spiritual movement in the Church today." For a history of the movement see the author's other books FROM A MORNING PRAYER and MEET THE WITNESSES. A free copy of the Blue Army's morning offering may be obtained from any of its centers.

BOSCO, St. John: This great saint of the last century, whose special vocation was helping wayward boys, made many prophesies which were fulfilled in his own lifetime, as well as many which have been fulfilled since. One of the most remarkable of these prophesies was made in 1862 foretelling the Ecumenical Council and the tempests which would precede and follow it. The Saint said that when the Pope succeeded in fastening the barque of Peter to the Pillars of the Eucharist and of Mary, the tempest would subside.

CANONIZED: A person is called "canonized" when the Pope, usually standing beneath the relic of the chair of Saint Peter and in the presence of the College of Cardinals, solemnly pronounces that this person is in heaven and worthy of veneration. The Greek word *Kanon* means a list, and the person proclaimed "saint" is officially "listed" among those in heaven. Three steps are necessary for such a listing: 1) The person's life is studied and must be found to have been marked by virtue to a *heroic* degree; 2) Then follows a much more detailed examination, which requires lengthy deposition of witnesses, study of all writings and works, examination of cult and miracles. If all is favorable, a person is declared "Blessed"; 3) Then two new miracles are required, plus a re-examination of the life, before the final solemn act of canonization. This not infrequently takes a century. It rarely takes less than fifty years, except in the case of martyrs. As an example, Blessed Anne Marie Taigi who performed many miracles in her own lifetime and was personally revered by several Popes, after a hundred years had still not been canonized.

CATACOMBS: Cemeteries under ground. The most famous are in and around Rome. So far over a hundred miles of tunnels, with graves on both sides, have been opened there. More are being opened at the present time. Already overwhelming evidence of the predominance of the Eucharist in the lives of early Christians has been brought to light as various photographs in this book bear witness. We may still expect more. Detailed documentation is available from the Pontifical Institute of Christian Archeology in Rome and from the Fabbrica di San Pietro, to both of which we are indebted for most of the photographs in this book.

CHALICE: A cup used in the Eucharistic Liturgy, usually gold (at least inside). It may be of any shape. The original chalice used by Our Lord at the last supper was known as the "Holy Grail" and was the object of fabled search in the middle ages. It is most often shaped like a goblet. Communion is given from a chalice in many instances. See ATHENAGORAS.

CHURCH: See FATHERS of the CHURCH.

COMMUNION: Naturally in discussing the Eucharist we must use this word frequently because it is the final purpose of the Eucharistic liturgy. It comes from the Greek word *koinonia* and is one of the key words of the theology of the Church, of Salvation, and of grace (See J. M. Tillard's *Pasch of God's People*, pg. 295). By the Covenant (see this word) and especially by the New Covenant concluded "in the Lord Jesus", we are united with God in all the dimensions of love, in *agape* (see this word). And this is what we mean by communion. By receiving the Eucharist we enter into union not only with God but also with each other in Him. The fruit of this "communion" is the Mystical Body (see this word), the Church.

CONSECRATED BREAD: see CONSECRATION.

CONSECRATION: In the Eucharistic Liturgy this word has a special meaning: It refers to the repetition of the actual words of Christ over bread and wine, by a duly ordained minister, so that transubstantiation (see this word) occurs. It is the most solemn moment in the Eucharistic Liturgy.

CORPORAL: Three altar cloths are required, plus a fourth small cloth which is placed just under the chalice and host. This latter is called a corporal. It is extra protection in the event that any consecrated wine might be spilled, or any particles of a consecrated host might be dropped. This corporal, or extra small altar cloth, is carefully guarded because it comes into direct contact with the Body of Christ. The priest cares for it personally.

COUNCIL: See TRENT and VATICAN II.

COVENANT: In Hebrew it is *berit;* in Greek *diatheke.* Our English word, from the Latin "to come together," means an agreement between two parties, or an agreement by one party based on certain conditions being fulfilled by the other. This latter is of course the meaning of the word in Scripture. First God made a covenant with the Jews on Mount Sinai, following the first Passover; then He made a new covenant with all men following the Passover which became the first Eucharistic Liturgy. In the first

Covenant He offers Himself to man on conditions of Justice. In the new covenant He offers Himself on conditions of *agape* (see this word), or love. The word "testament" is often used interchangeably with "covenant".

CRYPTOGRAPHY: From the Greek word for secret (kryptos): The act or art of writing in secret characters. This was a principal art and also a means of communication among the early Christians. Some of the secret symbols have only recently been deciphered as we have noted in chapter four.

DEPOSIT OF FAITH: The sum total of truths revealed by Christ, taught by the Church without error, and witnessed by Scripture and Tradition. Concerning the latter, we have the teaching of the Fathers. One of the marks of a Father of the Church, in addition to wisdom and a holy life and having lived in the early centuries, is that what he taught had the consensus of approval by all Christians. See FATHERS OF THE CHURCH.

EASTERN RITES: see ORTHODOX and ECUMENISM.

ECUMENICAL COUNCIL: See TRENT and VATICAN II.

ECUMENISM: Comes from a Greek word meaning "Inhabited world". We might translate it as "universalism". Until recent times it appeared only as an adjective (ecumenic, or ecumenical) but especially since Pope John XXIII the word has come to be very commonly used among all Christians as an attitude and effort towards unity of faith, hope, and love among all who confess Christ, the Lord, and even more generally among all who confess the Fatherhood of God. The Eucharist remains at the heart of ecumenism not only because it is the sacrament (see this word) of unity, but because *at its institution* Christ prayed for all: *"Father, that they may be one as You and I are*

One." All efforts at true Christian ecumenism remain peripheral until they arrive at the Eucharist, although that day of "arrival" may not be as close as many would like. The Patriarch of Constantinople, His Holiness Athenagoras I, powerful figure in the ecumenical movement, said: "I often have a vision when I look from my bedroom window: I see a beautiful hand holding the chalice of Our Lord over a nearby hill, and I hear secret voices that speak of love between humanity and peace among men . . . The responsibility for starting toward unity lies with the Christians". (Interview published in LIFE magazine, March 31, 1967). The vision of the venerable Patriarch, who is as revered in the Eastern Church as Pope John XXIII in the West, bears amazing similarity to the vision seen by the children of Fatima in 1916 described in Chapter XII of this book.

EMBRYO: The earliest formation of cells which will develop into a complete living being. When parts begin to develop it is called a fetus.

ENTELECHY: From Greek meaning *To complete*. Science at the present time does not know what properties in cells cause them to develop in a definite progress of complex multiplication to a single, whole living being. Since the word entelechy designates a conception completely actualized, in distinction from mere potential existence, we apply this word to what nevertheless remains unknown.

EUCHARIST: From the Greek word *eucharistia*: thanksgiving. The name refers to Christ under the form of bread and wine and is derived from the thanksgiving which Christ made to his Father just before pronouncing over bread "This is my body," and over wine "This is my blood."

EUCHARISTIC CHRIST: This term is actually redundant because the Eucharist *is* Christ. It's something like saying "The Christly Christ." But we use it to emphasize Christ in his hidden, sacramental form as distinguished from Christ as He is in Heaven or as He was in Palestine.

EUCHARISTIC CONGRESS:
These international assemblies have grown in importance with each passing year. There is perhaps no demonstration on earth that draws more persons, from more nations, in a prolonged act of Divine Worship. Lasting several days (the one in Bombay, India, in 1964, was attended by Pope Paul VI and lasted ten days) it consists of a series of Masses, hours and nights of adoration and reparation, sermons, studies and conferences, processions, etc., all aimed at honor to Our Lord in the Eucharist and of increasing Eucharistic devotion in the world. They have been held on every continent, and in most of the principal nations of the world. They take place every four years, as in Bogota, Columbia, in August, 1968, then in 1972, 1976, and so on.

EUCHARISTIC HEART OF JESUS: The heart of Jesus is a real part of his real body but it has been the object of special devotion through the ages, especially in modern times, *as representing the love of Christ for men*. For the history of the devotion see Aug. Hamon, S.J., *Histoire de la devotion au Sacre-Coeur*, published in Paris 1923-40, in five volumes, and for perhaps the best single work on the object, motives, and practice of the devotion; see *Devotion to the Sacred Heart*, by Louis Verheylesoon, S.J., publ. 1955 by Sand & Co., London (280 pp.), originally published in Flemish in 1946.

FAITH: See DEPOSIT of FAITH.

FATHERS OF THE CHURCH: The Christian Church was completely united for the first thousand years, and even the political separation between the East and West was not final until the fifteenth century. The doctrinal break came after Martin Luther, in the sixteenth. So the "Fathers" of the Church are common to all Christians and the title is applied to those great Christian teachers of the first centuries when Christians dared to come out in the open after the persecutions. These were the men who explained what Christ had taught even more fully than the gospels recorded. John had said that if all they had learned from Our Lord were recorded "Not even the world itself, I think, could hold the books that would have to be written" (John 21, 25). And Churchmen like Justin, Aristides, Origen, Clement of Alexandria, said far more than had ever been preached in public. But even before them were others like Ignatius, Clement and Polycarp (the latter an actual disciple of Saint John) who had recorded explanation and facts received directly from the apostles. And they all became witnesses (martyrs). Then as time passed there came Saint Augustine, St. Gregory the Great (sixth century), and finally the last doctor of the East: Saint John Damascene, at the very end of the centuries of secrecy. We consider what was taught by the "Fathers" as belonging to the deposit of faith left by the Apostles.

FATIMA: A town in central Portugal, 3,000 feet above sea level and about 80 miles north of Lisbon in the Serra d'Aire Mountains. It was an obscure mountain parish comprised of a scattering of very small villages until 1917 when three shepherd children here had a series of twelve apparitions: Six of angels, in 1916; six of the Blessed Virgin in 1917, climaxed by a miracle at a time and place predicted by the children "So that everyone may believe." The message given by these multiple visions is, in the words of Pope Pius XII: "An affirmation of the Gospel". There was nothing new except the apparitions themselves, and the miracle. The message covered just about every gospel doctrine: Heaven, Hell, sin, reparation, angelic messengers, the Eucharist, and above all daily duty; the acceptance of God's Will in all things. New stress was placed on devotion to the Blessed Virgin, as explained in Chapter XIV of this book, as a source of strength both for entering into the Gospel message and for living it. But the message itself was the Gospel message. Some say Fatima might be likened to Sinai. There was nothing new in the Ten Commandments, either, but the world had forgotten them. The Eucharistic character of the message of Fatima was not completely known until August, 1967, when a vision like the diagram(p.289)was made public for the first time. The vision actually took place in July, 1929, and was communicated to Pope Pius XI by letter. "It shows," says the Rev. Messias Coelho, Portuguese authority who revealed the letter to Pius XI, "that the message of Fatima is essentially Eucharistic." The words communicated to the world at the time of this vision were: "This is the last hour to make the consecration of Russia and the Communions of Reparation." Pope Pius XII made the consecration of Russia publicly in 1942, and appealed for Communions of Reparation. The vision strongly recalls the first apparition of Fatima: Christ appeared on the cross all in light, surmounted by representations of the Holy Spirit and the Father. Blood flowed from His side to a Host, and from the Host into a chalice, while Our Lady stood on the opposite side interceding with outstretched hands, her Immaculate Heart shown surrounded by thorns.

FIRST-FRIDAYS: They have to do with the most important of the promises made to Saint Margaret Mary Alacoque (see ALACOQUE) by Our Lord, when He appeared to her out of the monstrance (see this word) on July 2nd, 1874. He said: "First you are to receive Me in the Blessed Sacrament as often as obedience will allow, no matter what mortification or humiliation it may entail. Moreover, you are to receive Holy Communion on the First Friday of each month, and every night between Thursday and Friday I will make you a partaker of that sorrow unto death which it was My will to suffer in the Garden of Olives." Our Lord asked this in reparation (see this word) for the sins of men. Then, during the octave of the Feast of Corpus

Christi, in 1675, He appeared again. He said: "Behold this Heart which has so loved men that I spared nothing . . . And in return I receive from the greater part of men nothing but ingratitude, by the contempt, irreverence, sacrileges and coldness with which they treat Me in this Sacrament of Love." To those who would receive Him in Communion on nine consecutive First Fridays He promised the grace of a happy death.

FIRST-SATURDAYS: Although Marian acts of reparation on First Saturdays were encouraged by the Church before the apparitions of Fatima, they were dignified in 1917 with a promise from Heaven similar to that attached to the First Fridays (see this word). The blessed Virgin promised that those who would go to confession, say the Rosary, spend fifteen minutes in meditation on the mysteries of the Rosary and receive Holy Communion . . . all four acts with the intention of making reparation for the offenses committed against Her Immaculate Heart . . . would enjoy *her presence* at the hour of death, and a happy death, if they persevered in the devotion for five consecutive first Saturdays. Subsequently it has become a custom for many generous souls to begin with Mass of the Sacred Heart on First Friday night, spend the entire night in reparation before the Blessed Sacrament, ending with the Mass of the Immaculate Heart on the first Saturday morning. Thus they reply generously to the appeals for reparation made by Our Lord at Paray-le-Monial and by Our Lady at Fatima and they are sure to enjoy the fulness of the great promises made by the Hearts of Jesus and Mary to repair the sins (see this word) of the world. However less than an hour is actually needed to complete the essentials of the devotion on each of five First Saturdays.

FRIDAYS: See First Fridays.

GOD: We speak of Him so often in this book that it might

be proper, if somewhat daring, to try to define Him. But since that is what most of the entire science of theology (see this word) is about, we need say merely that He is BEING. He has no parts, as do creatures. But even geniuses have only a vague idea of what this BEING is because He is different from our kind of being. He is absolute Being and we have merely "contingent being." We can rationalize that He does not exist because we cannot understand *how we* can exist outside of Him. Anyone who has seen a miracle needs no rationalizing. Those who have not seen miracles can know of them from reliable witnesses. And those without excuses, and with common sense, just "know" they came from this BEING, Who is all Perfection, and that they are destined to enjoy Him.

HARRIS, Frank: A contemporary of De Maupassant, prominent in British journalism in the last century. The quotations here are from his autobiography published by Corgi, London, 1963, page 306. One of the prominent quotes used by the publisher in the introduction of this book describes Harris as "A dirty old man". Because of extreme pornography, the book was banned in the United States, like Henry Miller's work, for many years. However, contrary to the opinion expressed by the Englishman, it was never put on the Church index. Few books, which one's common sense warns against, ever are.

HERIS, CHARLES V., O.P., author of *L'Eucharistie, Mystere de Foi* published by Alsatia in Paris in 1967, 224 pages, distinguishes between physical substance and real substance, and Father Heris says it is a serious mistake to confound the two domains of physical science and of the creation-and-restoration, because the first is of the order of *human* science and the other introduces us to divine Science (capitalized) in which Christ places His word: "This is My Body . . ." Nowhere will the layman have greater difficulty in discussing the Eucharist with the metaphysician, or theologian, than in ths area where the difference in the meaning of words can become an almost insurmountable stumbling block. In our chapter on "Science and the Secret" we talk the layman's language, not the metaphysician's. And we do not attempt to explain the unexplainable. We merely show that, in the light of modern science, even if Christ's words were applied to matter *as it really is* there will be found to be NO CONTRADICTION in the limitation of Christ's "extension" or Body within the apparent confines of absolute accidents of bread and wine. For a scientist's comment on this, see HEYDEN below. Abbe Andre Richard, a friend of the author, who sought criticism of the French translation of this book, says:

"The explanation regarding scientific conceptions of today can perhaps be indicated as showing that beneath the appearances which fall upon the senses there is a specific and mysterious reality which is the basis of being, from which arises this or that quality of manifestation which our senses perceive.

"I have often given to children in catechism class the following image:

"Suppose God might suddenly annihilate the sun exactly at noon. We know that the sun's rays, the sun's light, the sun's heat, would all continue to arrive upon the earth for eight minutes. We would say: 'What a beautiful sun!' and in reality the sun would no longer be in existence. Then, suddenly, all would be dark.

"However, even if He did destroy the sun, God could by a miracle preserve the rays of the sun, with their light and heat, accomplishing by His direct Power what the sun did of its own nature.

"In a similar manner the 'rays' of the bread . . . that is its exterior qualities . . . can be preserved by God even though the substance of the bread has been removed and changed into the Presence of the Body of Christ."

See the word ACCIDENT.

HEYDEN, S.J., Dr. Francis J.: Director of Georgetown College Observatory and world famous scientist. He commented on Chapter VII: "It is true that the physical concept of matter today identifies it with energy inasmuch as the relation $E = mc^2$ has been verified both by fusion and fission. While most physicists also feel that what we call matter in the universe did condense from energy, they have not yet been able to demonstrate the reversal of energy into mass.

"Treating atoms as point forces, of course, goes back to the philosophers of the last century, Palmieri and Boscovitch, who described atoms as puncta inflata or inflated points, their doctrine of extension, by which quantity is measured, called it virtual in contrast to formal.

"Since no one can question either doctrine in cosmology as far as the mystery of transubstantiation is concerned, there is nothing wrong one way or the other with Chapter VII in *The World's Greatest Secret*. But since we speak of energy density as well as plain density for mass, some cosmologist might want to argue about formal and virtual extension. Call it either, you still have extension or partes extra partes.

"The chapter establishes with sufficient clarity the fact that faith alone provides us with the information that the Real Presence exists after consecration under the appearances of bread and wine.

"How small a quantity must one have before one can have the Real Presence in consecration? I have never figured that out. I have always believed that perhaps the angels have to gather up the tiny flecks that fall or blow away while a priest gives communion."

HOLY SPIRIT: see TRINITY.

HOST: From the Latin word for *hostage, applied to Christ* as the victim for our sins. This usage appears in the prayers of the Mass. But then it was applied to the Eucharist and in particular to the consecrated bread. It is sometimes improperly used to refer to the bread used for the Eucharist even before consecration (see this word).

INCARNATION: From the Latin meaning "to become flesh." This is the word for the belief expressed by Christians in the ancient Nicene Creed: "I believe in one Lord, Jesus Christ, the only-begotten Son of God . . . of one substance with the Father . . . Who for us men and for our salvation came down from heaven. *And He became flesh* by the Holy Spirit of the Virgin Mary: and was made man."

IMMACULATE CONCEPTION: Contrary to somewhat common belief, this term has nothing to do with the fact that Mary was a Virgin. It means that from the moment of her conception she was sinless in anticipation of the merits of Christ's redemption. In other words, she was redeemed by Our Lord like all other humans, but God gave her special graces and immunity from sin (since she was to provide us with the Body of Christ) in virtue of the redemption which would follow. She was born, like Adam and Eve, sinless and in union with God. Thus she could become "the new Eve," as several Fathers of the Church refer to her. See Fathers of the Church.

IMMACULATE HEART: Since the first drop of Christ's Blood came, in a manner of speaking, from the heart of Mary, it was fitting that her heart should have been all pure. But, as in devotion to the Sacred Heart (see this term), this term refers to the Blessed Virgin in her entirety. The word "immaculate" emphasizes what Mary means to us who lost grace through our first parents. She is, as the Protestant poet Wordsworth exclaimed: "Our tainted nature's solitary boast". Most of the world's population (including Mohammedans) believe that she was immaculate, or sinless. Devotionally (as we explain in Chapter XIV) we try to apply this immaculateness to ourselves that we may the more worthily, confidently, easily plunge ourselves into the Sacred Heart of Christ.

LATERAN, Saint John: When Christians emerged from the catacombs, Constantine gave to Peter's successor the so-called Lateran Palace to be converted to church use and it thus became the first principal church of the Christian world. To this day, it is so designated. Over its main portal is inscribed the phrase: *Omnium urbis et orbis ecclesiarum mater et caput,* "The Mother and Head of all the churches of the city and of the world." Because of its venerable character and importance, the Pope celebrates the Eucharistic Liturgy here on Holy or Maundy Thursday. A major relic of the church is considered part of the table of the Last Supper. For the Passover, the Jews did not sit at table as at ordinary meals, but reclined around it on low divans. The famous painting by Da Vinci is imaginary.

LITURGY: From the Greek, *leitourgia,* a public service. It refers to the official worship of God through the Church accomplished in three major ways: 1) Through the Eucharistic Sacrifice; 2) the recitation of official prayers known as "the Divine Office"; 3) the administration of the Sacraments and the annexed use of the sacramentals. *Catholic Dictionary* (Grosset and Dunlap, 1965, pg. 342) says: "The culmination of the liturgy is the Eucharist because here the encounter with Christ is *personal and very real,* the closest contact that can be obtained with Christ and salvation." But an important aspect of *liturgy* is the word "public." It is not a solitary, individual act. We participate in the liturgy as members of the Mystical Body of Christ, as members of His Church. Not only do we share in the love of Christ for the Father, but there is a force in the liturgy which enables us to share in His love for mankind and to love our neighbor as we love God. This aspect was strongly emphasized in the *Constitution on the Sacred Liturgy* issued by Vatican Council II on Dec. 4, 1963.

LUTHER, Martin: He was an Augustinian friar who on Oct. 31, 1517, launched the Protestant Reformation. Many feel that if John XXIII had been Pope, or if it had been 1967 instead of 1517, Luther would not have separated from Rome. But he did, and he taught (in defense of his own divergence) the right of private judgment. So subsequent divisions in Christianity have come to be numbered in the hundreds. Dr. Kent S. Knutson, Director of Graduate Studies at the Luther Theological Seminary in Saint Paul, Minnesota, was consulted in reference to our quotation from Luther in Chapter VII. The statement we quoted appears in *Wider Etliche Tollen Geister,* but Dr. Knutson says: "You might quote a better known and more substantial work, such as the confession concerning Christ's Supper, of 1528, or *This Is My Body* where he says that 'These words of Christ, *This is My Body,* etc., still stand firm against the fanatics', written in 1527. There is never a question in the mind of Luther about the doctrine of the real presence."

MAKHLOUF, Blessed Charbel: A Lebanese Maronite Monk of the Monastery of Annaya, which is about a two hour drive by private car from Beirut, over 4,000 feet above sea level. He died in 1898, seventy years of age, after a life of incredible austerity. During the last twenty-three years he lived in an unheated hermitage, even without glass at the window and with the stone floor as his bed although the temperature much of the year was well below freezing. His devotion to the Holy Mass was so great that he finally asked permission to spend his entire life just in preparing for Mass and making thanksgiving each day. Through the most extraordinary miracles, including the miracle of the preservation of his body and the constant emission of fluid from the incorrupt body, the attention of the world was drawn to his Eucharistic life. The few details quoted in this book are known to the writer at first hand. He was present at the beatification of Blessed Charbel in St. Peter's

Basilica in Rome on May 12, 1965, and examined much of the documentation, garments, samples of blood, etc., in the company of Father Touvia Ciade, present Superior of the Convent at Annaya, on the Feast of Corpus Christi, 1967.

MARTYR: From the Greek word meaning "witness." We use it to refer to a person who has died for his faith. But the early Christians used it to denote a person who, by giving his life, bore witness to the proof of Christ's resurrection and of the Eucharistic and other doctrines he had taught them. See WITNESS.

MARY: See IMMACULATE CONCEPTION and IMMACULATE HEART.

MASS: From the Latin "missa", at the end of the Eucharistic Liturgy. Because of its brevity the word has been commonly applied to the entire Eucharistic Liturgy but new stress has been placed on the full title since Vatican Council II. The words *Ite missa est* at the end of the liturgy mean: "Depart, it is ended."

MAUNDY THURSDAY: From the Latin "to wash," referring to the washing of feet before the Eucharistic liturgy. It takes place on the Thursday before good Friday and recalls that this was how Christ opened the first Eucharistic liturgy the night before He died.

MESSIAH: In Hebrew it means "Anointed," and it was used in Israel to designate the expected king (the anointed one) who would deliver Israel and be the Saviour of his people. See SAVIOUR.

MILLER, Henry, materialistic contemporary writer, of the De Maupassant "school", whose books were wide source of controversy because of pornographic passages. His own best selling book he described as a "Kick in the pants of God." It often reflects sloughs of despondency into which materialists logically fall and to which we refer here.

MIRACLE: The word here is used in its strict sense . . . not of something which is merely surprising, but something *above and beyond the powers of nature.* Some say that there are no miracles, just no explanations. But that shows a lack of understanding of what we mean by the word: We mean an act or event above and beyond the KNOWN and EXPLAINED laws of nature, such as five thousand men being fed with food that was insufficient for five, or the instantaneous appearance of dry scars where there had been open, draining fistulas one moment before. By the word "miracle" we mean something which any rational person, with adequate knowledge of cause and effect, can attribute only to God.

MONSTRANCE: From the Latin "To Show." This is a sacred vessel used to display the Eucharist for adoration. It is usually gold, often decorated with precious stones with rays emanating from a glass in the center beneath which the Sacred Host is reserved. During the Forty Hours devotion (see reference to Bl. John Newman in chapter XIII) the monstrance is used, as well as for the ceremony of blessing with the Eucharist known as Benediction. In recent years, thousands of persons have been spending entire nights before the Blessed Sacrament exposed in a monstrance in petition and reparation. This is called the "All Night Vigil."

MOUNT ZION, or Mount Sion, is the mountain on which Jerusalem was built and on which King David was buried. Here Jews and Christians have holy places in common: The tomb of King David and the traditional location of the "upper room" or "cenacle" which Christ celebrated the Passover the night before He died and instituted the Eucharist. It is also the room in which the Paraclete came upon the disciples.

MYSTERY: This book uses this word in its restricted sense

of something which cannot be wholly understood. Some mysteries of life are only temporary; we may get to understand them with increased knowledge. But the Eucharist is a mystery which we not only cannot understand now, but will never wholly understand because to do so we would have to understand the Incarnation (see this word) and this would in turn require an understanding of the nature of God Himself which is beyond our scope. There arrives a point at which, in the words of the great scholastic genius, Thomas Aquinas, we must say: "I believe because Christ, who is Truth, told me." We believe not because we understand, but because it is unreasonable not to believe. Despite all the facts and all the miracles, the mystery remains. Still we can be dazzled by passages of the SUMMA THEOLOGICA of Saint Thomas Aquinas, especially in Part III, questions 79 and 80, of which Tillard says: "Here the great optimism of living Tradition about the redemptive value of the Eucharistic body and blood vibrates to the fullest."

MYSTICAL BODY: It is important not to mistake the word "mystical" which means *hidden,* with the word "mythical," which means *fable.* Christ, at the first Eucharistic Liturgy, said that now Christians . . . united to each other by communion with Him (in the actual consumption of Him under the forms of bread and wine) . . . were like branches of a vine: "I am the vine, you are the branches" (John 15, 5). Now all Christians became joined in His Body into One Body. This body cannot be seen, except in its individual members. But it is a *real* body. The doctrine was explained by Pope Pius XII in a magnificent encyclical: *Mystici Corporis.*

MYSTICISM: Communion between two lovers is visible in sighs, words, deeds. Communion between the soul and God is often invisible, and is therefore called "mystic" or secret. "Mysticism" refers primarily to the very highest form of communion with God. It means a very real experience of God's presence in the soul which often results in definite physiological or psychological manifestations, such as freedom from gravity (levitation), radiance, inexplicable fragrances, stigmata, etc. Such manifestations are not always present, but in modern usage a "mystic" is usually thought to be a person in such close communion with God that such manifestations are evident. Therese Neumann, to whom we refer here and who lived for years solely on the Eucharist, was a well known mystic of recent times. All the mystics of Christian history seem to have centered their lives on the Blessed Sacrament.

NEUMANN, THERESA: See MYSTICISM.

NICENE CREED: This is the common ground of almost all Christians. It was composed in the Council of Nicaea in 325, immediately after the age of persecutions, to publicly state major truths of the Church which might be called into question. Since the Eucharist was still the "Christian Secret," and perhaps also because it was the unquestioned center of Christian faith, it was not included in the Creed. At the time of the Council of Nicaea, the Eucharist was universally the center of Christian life and faith.

ORTHODOX: When we use this term we are referring to the Eastern Church. It was a collective name for self-governing churches of eastern Europe and western Asia. Most of these churches, under the Patriarch of Constantinople, separated from Rome in 1054 largely because of political differences. Their manner of celebrating the Eucharistic liturgy differs from most western churches (as it has from earliest times), but doctrinal differences are few. The Patriarch of Constantinople in 1967 referred to the Pope of Rome as "My brother Paul" and said: "We must now eliminate through ecclesiastical acts those elements which divide us". Most Russians are to be counted among the

160,000,000 Orthodox Catholics. They have a valid priesthood, valid sacraments, and consequently the true Eucharist.

OUR LADY OF THE BLESSED SACRAMENT: This is the title of an excellent booklet of prayers published by St. Peter Julian Eymard's Congregation (Fathers of the Blessed Sacrament). Although the prayers are especially written for the nine days preceding May 13th, Feast of Our Lady of the Blessed Sacrament, they may be used at any time. In the United States the booklet is published by the Sentinel Press, 194 East 76th St., New York 10021. There are three major reasons cited for the devotion to the Blessed Virgin under the title of "Our Lady of the Blessed Sacrament": 1) The body of Our Lord, received in Communion, was born of Mary; 2) Grace comes through Mary, and especially the greatest of all graces, the Eucharist; 3) The life of the Blessed Virgin after the ascension of Our Lord (when she lived with St. John) models for us the relationship we should have in our own lives to Christ in the Eucharist.

PASCH: The Hebrew word is *pesah*, or passover. It is a Jewish feast commemorating the deliverance of the Israelites from Egyptian slavery. See PASSOVER.

PASSOVER: From the words *pass* and *over*, referring to the fact that the angel of death passed over those houses which were sprinkled with the blood of the lamb and thus led to the great *passage* of the Jews from the slavery of Egypt to freedom and the promised land. Aphraates draws the comparison between the original Passover, the Last Supper, and the new covenant: "On the Passover the Jews escaped from the slavery of Pharaoh; on the day of the Crucifixion we were delivered from the slavery of Satan. They sacrificed a lamb whose blood saved them from the exterminator; we were delivered by the Blood of the well-beloved Son from our works of corruption. They had Moses for a guide; we have Jesus for Head and Saviour.

For them Moses divided the sea and had them cross; our Saviour opened the depths and broke their gates when, descending into the depths he opened them and forged the way at the head of all those who were to believe in him (Dem., 12, 8). J. M. Tillard, O.P., in *The Eucharist, Pasch of God's People* (Alba House, 1967) develops this point at length.

PRESANCTIFICATION: This refers to the passage described by Saint Luke: "When Elizabeth heard the greeting of Mary the babe in her womb leapt. And Elizabeth cried out with a loud voice, saying: 'Blessed art thou among women and blessed is the fruit of thy womb! And how have I deserved that the mother of my Lord should come to me? For behold, the moment that the sound of thy greeting came to my ears the babe in my womb leapt for joy.' " (Luke 1, 41) It is understood that this was, in a sense, the moment of baptism for the child of Elizabeth who was himself to become the baptiser, the herald of Christ. Hence the word "presanctification," or sanctification before birth.

REFORMATION: See LUTHER.

REPARATION: This is an important word in the modern world. Great stress was placed on it in the messages of Fatima and Lourdes. If enough good persons make reparation, the world was told at Fatima (see this word) that God will obtain peace among all men. But if reparation is not made (obviously by those who believe for those who do not believe), communism and allied errors will spread through the entire world and provoke further wars, ultimately "entire nations will be annihilated." Reparation means simply "Repairing." To understand it we need merely to understand the meaning of sin (see this word).

ROSETTA STONE: Despite years of effort to decipher the hieroglyphics of ancient Egypt, no one succeeded until recent times when a trilingual stone was found in the town of Rosetta. This stone gave archeologists the key to understanding hieroglyphics and thus unlocked countless facts of the ancient world, facts previously unknown altogether or else the object of mere guesswork.

SACRAMENT: Originally the Latin word meant any "sacred thing", but in the Church, today, a sacrament means only those seven things made particularly sacred by Christ: Marriage (at Cana); the Eucharist and the Priesthood (at the Last Supper and after the Resurrection); last rites for the dying (as on Calvary); Baptism; Confirmation (sending of the Paraclete); Penance ("What you shall bind upon earth," etc.). And these seven sacred things bear the Presence of Christ within them, although He is physically present only in the Eucharist which is therefore called the *Blessed Sacrament*. Other instruments of God's help, not directly instituted by Christ and not containing grace as it were within themselves, are called "little sacraments" or "sacramentals". Among the most celebrated of the latter are rosaries, scapulars, representations of Christ and the saints, and so on. In Catechism, a sacrament is defined as an outward sign of inward grace, instituted by Christ.

SACRED HEART: This is an endearing and reverential term for *Christ Himself*, even as the term "dear heart" might refer to any beloved person. The term refers to the entire Christ because the heart is the symbol of love and Christ is Love itself (Card. Franzelin, S.J., *De Verbo Incarnato*, cap. vi. tesis xiv.). The great Vermeersch, whom we have delighted to quote in others of our books, points out that the Heart of Christ is not taken like a metaphor, but as the real and natural *symbol* of Christ's love (Vol. II, pg. 33, *Pratique et doctrine de la devotion au Sacre Coeur*, Tournai, 1930).

SACRIFICE: The Eucharist must be seen in two lights: As a Sacrament (see this word), and Sacrifice, which means an offering of expiation. As we explain in the text, the

Eucharistic Liturgy *makes the sacrifice of Calvary present.* But neither aspect (sacrament or sacrifice) *is ever actually separate.* The Eucharist is the sacrament of the sacrificial act of Christ. "Communion," says Tillard (op. cit., pg. 313), "with the consecrated bread is intended only to render us participants in the sacrifice of the Pasch of Jesus; the bread and wine are consecrated to render sacramentally present this paschal sacrifice." We perhaps can appreciate this if we place ourselves in the position of Saint John at the last Supper . . . resting his head on the very breast of Christ, feeling His Heart beat . . . and then within a matter of hours standing at the foot of His cross. To us a single Communion is all this. The very word "Host" means victim. The Eucharist unites me to my Saviour, and my Saviour to me.

SAINT: See CANONIZED.

SATURDAYS: See First Saturdays.

SECRET OF THE MASS: That part of the Mass just after the recitation of the Nicene Creed which prepares for the consecration (see this word) when transubstantiation (see this word) will occur. In the early church, anyone who had not been baptized and confirmed was not allowed to remain in church when this sacred part of the Liturgy began. In the Oriental rites, even to this day, the priest cries out just before this sacred part: "The doors, the doors, attention to the doors". Some writers suggest that this part was called "Secret" because the priest said the prayers in a low voice. But, as we have shown extensively in these pages, this sacred part of the Eucharistic liturgy was indeed a secret . . . which means of course something hidden from the uninitiated. The use of the term lost meaning after the early centuries of persecution, but to this day many (especially non-Christians) are amazed to discover this "Secret" of Christians. Vatican Council II removed the word "Secret" and substituted the words "Liturgy of the Eucharist". The sacred prayers are now said aloud (since Vatican Council II) so that all can hear.

SIN: Can be described in various ways, but essentially it is disobedience to God Who is All Goodness. It is the free choice of personal indulgence in a matter contrary to the law of God, whether that law be manifest through legitimate authority or through principles evident in creation. Its gravity depends especially on the knowledge and motivation of the sinner. An act wrong in itself is not a sin if the person performing it does not recognize it as sinful, i.e., as contrary to the will of God. The extent of the evil in the first sin, committed by a man and a woman who enjoyed intimacy with God and an abundance of intelligence and light, can hardly be understood by those who have never enjoyed such Divine intimacy. It required a supreme act of love on the part of God to restore man to the intimacy which the first man and woman had voluntarily renounced. The Eucharist is the perpetuation of that supreme act of God's love: the Incarnation. It follows (as taught by the angel of Fatima) that the best way of repairing for the sins of men is adoration, love, and offering of the Blessed Sacrament to the Most Holy Trinity.

SUBSTANCE: From Latin words meaning *stand under*. We use it in this book, in reference to transubstantiation, in a restricted sense of "that which makes a thing what it is," or rather that which is *real* rather than that which is *apparent*. It is the abiding part of any existence as distinguished from visible parts which may change, like color, shape, texture, etc. A table, for instance, is a table regardless of how many legs it has, what color or size it is, etc. The *substance* of a table is *that which makes it what it is*. See ACCIDENT and HERIS, CHARLES V., O.P.

TABERNACLE: Between celebrations of the Eucharistic liturgy, the Eucharist, or Sacred Species, is reserved in a boxlike structure known as a tabernacle. The word comes from ancient times. During the Exodus it was a portable box, with curtains, in which the Jews put the tablets of the commandments. This became the sacred place in the great temple of Jerusalem and was considered the *place of God's most intimate presence among His people*. Today there are churches all over the world where Christ is present Eucharistically in tabernacles, before which burns a red light as a sign of His presence. The original tabernacle from the time of Moses has been lost.

TESTAMENT: See COVENANT.

THEOLOGIANS: Those who study theology (see this word) whether ascetical, dogmatic, moral, mystical, natural, pastoral, or positive. Usually we think of the theologian as a student of all branches, but particularly *dogmatic,* which deals with truths of what we must believe about God. It is complex and requires a vast amount of other knowledge as well as spiritual sensitivity. Hence there are very few *great* theologians. They come from two schools: The Alexandrian and Antiochan, the first growing out of Platonic philosophy, the second from Aristotle. In the debates which raged between them during the early centuries, a clearer view of God began to emerge. Today the leading theologian of the past who is most invoked as an authority in reference to the matter of this book is Saint Thomas Aquinas. Some new, great theologians are arising today out of the ferment of thought exposed by Vatican Council II. The writer of this book skimmed many relevant theological works. He wanted to retain the simple layman's point of view while at the same time ascertaining that this view should not be without consciousness of the best professional opinions. (See SUBSTANCE).

THEOLOGY: Many have the false notion that theology is just a study of religion. Actually theology is a science, and perhaps the highest of all sciences because its object is the highest: God (see this word). Like any science, it is a study that proceeds from the known to the unknown and its primary method is to doubt and question and to seek incontrovertible answers. Because of its scientific method, theologians in general tend to be disputacious. There is so little about God of which we *are* certain that, as in philosophy, we find ourselves following the best minds or the majority of minds on those questions which are not dogmatic. It is the right of the theologian, the scientist of God, to question. It is perhaps also a right for simple layfolk to be spared their arguments. See THEOLOGIANS.

TRADITION: See FATHERS of the CHURCH.

TRANSUBSTANTIATION: This is a key word to understanding the Eucharist. It was strongly confirmed by Pope Paul VI in the encyclical published in this book, and by the Council of Trent (see pages 877, 884 of the *Enchiridion* published in Freiburg in 1953, by Denzinger, Bannwart, Umberg, and Rahner). It is a word which means literally what it implies: A transfer of substances. What was the substance of bread becomes the substance of Christ, whole and entire, body and blood and soul and divinity. All that remains of the bread are the absolute accidents of color, size, texture: that which is visible. See SUBSTANCE and ACCIDENT.

TRENT: At the height of the Protestant "revolt" the Bishops of the world assembled in this Austrian town to answer questions which had never before been seriously raised by Christians. There had been earlier councils, but this was the most important because the divisions of Protestantism brought about the first major break in the doctrinal unity of Christians. The Bishops, who met in December, 1545, were convened (off and on) for eighteen years. They confirmed the Nicene Creed and "defined" the Real Presence and Transubstantiation as its mode. They also declared that holy communion in both kinds was not necessary for those not celebrating because Christ is whole and entire under both species. They based their definitions on what had been taught since the time of Our Lord, as well as on reason and universality of belief among Christians transmitted by tradition and documents. Convened only 28 years after Martin Luther nailed his ninety-five theses on the doors of the church at Wittemberg, the Council affirmed (at least on the Eucharist) what nearly all Christians, including Martin Luther, had believed up to this time.

TRINITY: From Latin meaning Three-One. It is an aspect of the nature of God which we would not know if Christ had not told us during the first Eucharistic liturgy. This revelation was a further testimony of His love. He wanted us to know, in a sense, what God is like inside: Love so powerful that in loving Himself He becomes Himself again; returning the love He again becomes Himself. Loving, He is the Father; Loved, He is the Son; Loving between Father and Son He is the Holy Spirit. Yet He remains One, Simple, Absolute Being. As the Father He sent Himself into the world; as the Son He saved men and transubstantiated Himself to remain with us in the Eucharist; as the Paraclete He comes to enable us to return His love. (See GOD.)

VATICAN II, Ecumenical Council: Opened October 11, 1962, by Pope John XXIII with 2,540 council fathers. It ended Dec. 8, 1962, and reconvened under Pope Paul VI on September 29th, 1963, during which the Constitution on the Sacred Liturgy was adopted. The third session closed on Nov. 21st with a consecration of the world, and in particular of Russia, to the Immaculate Heart of Mary by Pope Paul in the presence of all the Council Fathers. Our Lady of Fatima had prophesied this as a sign of the "conversion of Russia." The final sessions in 1964 and 1965 dealt with the nature of the Church and ecumenism. The author wrote this book in Rome during most of the Council, and was present in Saint Peter's on Dec. 7th, 1965, when the last votes were cast and a Legate of Patriarch Athenagoras I, head of the 160,000,000-member-Orthodox-Church, read in the presence of the Council the lifting of the interdict against Rome, while the Secretary of the Council read a similar proclamation lifting the interdict against the Eastern Church. All the Bishops of the world broke into spontaneous applause as the Legate of the Eastern Church walked in solemn procession around the tomb of Peter. Our only quotation in this book from the Constitution on the Sacred Liturgy is from Rush, which is an early translation, but we used it because it coincides with the quotation in the Encyclical of Pope Paul which we quote in full in the appendix; several fine translations of the Vatican Council II documents are now available like the paperback published by America Press (An Angelus Book), with notes and comments by Catholic, Protestant and Orthodox authorities. The sixteen texts promulgated by the Council run to 103,014 words. Many of them may be forgotten but the effect of the Council on the union of the Eastern and Western Churches and on the final union of all Christians is materializing as the Council's (and Pope John's) twentieth century "miracle".

VIRGIN: It seems to have become customary among all Christians to refer to the Mother of Christ as "The Virgin," or the "Blessed Virgin," perhaps because such was the first reference to her by Saint Luke: " ... *To a virgin*, betrothed to a man named Joseph (1, 28); and in Matthew: "Now all this came to pass that what was spoken by the Lord through the prophet might be fulfilled. 'Behold *the virgin* shall be with child and shall bring forth a son; and they shall call his name Emmanuel', which is interpreted 'God with us'." (1, 22) Devotionally it is more proper to refer to her as "Mother" because in consenting to become the mother of Christ she became the mother of His whole body, and His Mystical Body (see this word). She has appeared on earth several times in the past century with the air of an anxious mother.

WITNESS: Comes from an Anglo-Saxon word meaning "To Know." It means attestation of a fact or event, or testimony to a truth. Many witnesses of the past are inert, like the inscriptions on the tombs of the first Christians. Other witnesses, equally silent but eloquent, are those who gave their lives rather than expose the truth to ridicule (like Tarcisius, see Chapter XIII).

BOOKS BY THE SAME WRITER which might be of particular interest to readers of THE WORLD'S GREATEST SECRET:

MEET THE WITNESS, AMI Press, 1961, 160pp.
> In 1959, after some fifty visits to Fatima, John Haffert sought living witnesses of the miracle of the sun which took place on October 13th, 1917. He obtained affidavits from witnesses in every walk of life, some on the verge of death. Sixty photographs buttress this documentation of a miracle performed in our own day, at a predicted time and place, "So that everyone may believe."

THIS HEAVENLY WORLD, AMI Press, 1966, 300pp.
> Of particular interest is the coverage of the Eucharistic Congress in Bombay, in 1964, and the stories of Bolsena-Orvieto and Santarem which are alluded to in Chapter VIII (Proofs). This book is a travelogue, with many pictures, edited by the author from CATHOLIC TRAVELER.

QUEEN'S PROMISE, AMI Press, 1966, 95pp.
> This is a synopsis of earlier books, *Russia Will Be Converted*, with some material from *Meet the Witnesses*. It is an authoritative account of the story and message of Fatima including a complete description of the Eucharistic apparition.

NIGHT OF LOVE, AMI Press, 1967, 176 pp.
> Book for All-night vigils.

OTHER BOOKS BY THE SAME AUTHOR —

RUSSIA WILL BE CONVERTED, AMI Press, 1952, 270pp.
> Became best-seller in its field.

FROM A MORNING PRAYER, AMI Press (new edition) 1961, 189pp.
> This is an autobiography and also became a best-seller. It might be of interest to some readers of THE WORLD'S GREATEST SECRET. It is mentioned in Chapter VI.

A LETTER FROM LISIEUX, AMI Press (new edition), 1965, 120pp.

MARY IN HER SCAPULAR PROMISE, AMI Press, new edition, 1954.
> Catholic book club selection.   Became best-seller in its field (over 100.000 copies).